Arlington, Virginia: Historical Guide for Travelers

American Cities History Guidebook Series

Henry Church

Published by Northwood Lore Books, 2023.

While every precaution has been taken in the preparation of this book, the publisher assumes no responsibility for errors or omissions, or for damages resulting from the use of the information contained herein.

ARLINGTON, VIRGINIA: HISTORICAL GUIDE FOR TRAVELERS

First edition. September 22, 2023.

Copyright © 2023 Henry Church.

ISBN: 979-8223002673

Written by Henry Church.

Also by Henry Church

American Cities History Guidebook Series
Charlottesville, Virginia: Historical Guide for Travelers
Williamsburg, Virginia: Historical Guide for Travelers
Richmond, Virginia: Historical Guide for Travelers
Norfolk & Virginia Beach: Historical Guide for Travelers
Winchester, Virginia: Historical Guide for Travelers
Baltimore, Maryland: Historical Guide for Travelers
Dover, Delaware: Historical Guide for Travelers
Arlington, Virginia: Historical Guide for Travelers

Table of Contents

Introduction

Picture yourself opening the cover of this book and walking down the historic streets of Arlington, Virginia. Here, the voices of soldiers, spies, politicians, and everyday heroes who have shaped this community and shaped the greater American story seem to be carried by every whisper of the wind. Arlington is a city full of lessons to teach and tales to tell; it is more than just a setting in the drama that is American history.

Learning about Arlington's past is like trying to piece together a complicated jigsaw puzzle; every piece, whether it be a historic conflict, a prominent citizen, or a game-changing piece of legislation, has a distinct meaning. However, we are only able to fully understand the tableau when these parts are put together. We will start by examining the land's Native American heritage, then examine its inclusion in George Washington's initial Federal District, and lastly examine its current use as a center for information technology and national defense. We'll vividly bring to life names like Robert E. Lee, who lived in what is now Arlington National Cemetery, and contextualize him in a way that goes beyond time and place.

Instead of following a straight path, our tour will zigzag across several historical periods to demonstrate the ways in which Arlington's past continues to influence its current social, cultural, and economic fabric. The region has experienced remarkable changes, from housing vital Civil War forts to being the center of the country's defense system, with the Pentagon serving as a symbol of both its military might and architectural prowess. The historical and contemporary significance of locations like the Air Force Memorial, Arlington National Cemetery, and the numerous IT businesses that have been nurtured here will be examined.

But without its people, what would Arlington be? We will explore the diverse range of communities that define Arlington, from African American communities that spawned vibrant neighborhoods like Freedman's Village to Civil War refugees and New Deal policymakers, to the influx of young professionals and foreign expatriates who add to the vibrant energy of the region. These varied groups have shaped public policy, contributed to social causes, shaped Arlington's culture, and encouraged innovation across a range of industries.

Our goal in weaving together the strands of the past and present is to offer a thorough grasp of how the city has changed over time and how its significant historical events have influenced the modern environment. Knowing the past of Arlington helps us to make more informed decisions about its future, whether it be in regards to urban growth, the area's economic prospects, or critical dialogues about social justice and equality.

Therefore, this book hopes to serve as your knowledgeable guide, be you a resident hoping to delve deeper into your community's history, a tourist seeking to discover one of America's most overlooked historical sites, or an inquisitive reader hoping to comprehend the many intricate details that make Arlington a microcosm of the country as a whole. Let's set out on this fascinating journey together and uncover the historical facets that make Arlington, Virginia, a national treasure full of undiscovered gems and priceless lessons.

Chapter 1: Native Tribes of Arlington

It's important to recognize Arlington, Virginia's original residents as you start your exploration—the Native American tribes that lived here for a very long time before European settlers ever set eyes on these lush hills and winding rivers. Before the area became the busy freeways and tall government buildings that define modern-day Arlington, it was a peaceful patchwork of open spaces, ponds, and woodlands that was abundant in wildlife. The Native American tribes that once lived in this region depended on the Potomac River, which you may pass on your daily commute. They believed that every sound made by leaves rustling and river ripples had a purpose within a complex ecology. It is within this framework that we start our exploration of Arlington's past.

The Dogue and Nacotchtank tribes, among other Algonquian-speaking peoples, were the main inhabitants of the area that is now Arlington. These tribes were nomadic, dwelling in towns or settlements frequently found next to the many rivers and streams in the region. The terrain, the waterways, and the seasons all had a profound impact on their way of life. The Potomac River served as more than just a river; it was a food supply, a trading route, and a holy place.

These tribes lived mostly off of agriculture, hunting, and fishing. The Nacotchtank and Dogue were expert fishermen who employed a variety of gear, including simple fishing lines and weirs. There was an abundance of fish, particularly sturgeon and shad, throughout their seasonal migrations. Deer, turkey, and smaller animals such as squirrels were hunted for their meat as well as their hides. Furthermore, the tribes were skilled farmers who produced crops like squash, beans, and maize (corn), which are collectively known as the "Three Sisters" due to their propensity to flourish when planted in tandem. Because of how successful these farming methods were, European settlers eventually adopted them, albeit with differing levels of awareness and reverence for the soil.

Like many other Native American tribes, their cosmology placed a high value on the natural environment, and spirituality was profoundly ingrained in daily life. There were many myths and symbolic meanings associated with plants, animals, and celestial bodies that helped to explain the mysteries of life. Stories were a common way for these stories to be passed down through the generations. The words of elders were venerated because they were thought to be the guardians of wisdom, both spiritual and practical.

The tribes that spoke Algonquian were a part of a wider network that involved trade, alliances, and occasionally confederations with other tribes. Stone tools, clay ceramics, woven baskets, and other products were traded, resulting in the development of a complex economic structure that stretched well beyond what is now known as Arlington. Archaeological digs in the region have turned up flint from far-off quarries, seashells from the Atlantic Coast, and copper from the Great Lakes, demonstrating the extensive reach of Native American trading lines.

Nonetheless, the advent of European explorers and colonists in the early 17th century brought about significant changes to this beautiful way of life. The original tribes suffered greatly as a result of the fast growing number of settlers, their new diseases, and their insatiable thirst for land, even though there may have initially been some trading and friendly engagement. By the late 17th century, the aboriginal tribes in this area were virtually vanished due to sickness, forced relocations, and acts of murder.

The tale of the Native American tribes who initially settled in Arlington is one of coexistence with the natural world and a sobering reminder of the negative effects of colonialism. It's worthwhile to pause and pay tribute to the original occupants of this land whether you're driving down the George Washington Memorial Parkway or strolling through one of Arlington's well-kept parks. Even though they are no longer the dominant culture here, their deep spirituality, love with the land, and intricate social systems nevertheless provide priceless insights. In order to remember those who came before us and live in closer harmony with the earth, their legacy challenges us to think about how we may do the same.

Gaining an understanding of Arlington's Native American heritage is essential to understanding the region's complicated and frequently turbulent past. It is the first crucial piece in our complex puzzle, a narrative strand that will be interwoven with the other chapters to create the rich tapestry that is Arlington, Virginia's historical identity.

Chapter 2: Early Settlers and Their Stories

Turning the pages of Arlington's history will reveal that the European era of exploration and settlement was a pivotal moment that profoundly altered the environment, both literally and figuratively. The story picks up speed to introduce a fresh group of people to the new location, each of them with hopes, dreams, and a very distinct perspective. However, it is impossible to observe the early settlers' imprints without also noting the erasure of the aboriginal people that had inhabited this territory. This dichotomy contains the intricate story of Arlington's early settlers.

Virginia was originally visited by European explorers in the early 17th century, one of the most well-known of whom was Captain John Smith. Smith encountered Native American tribes like the Dogue, who spoke Algonquian, while exploring the Chesapeake Bay and the Potomac River. The lush terrain and advantageous location of what would eventually become Arlington were not missed on these settlers, even if the early exploration effort was concentrated farther southeast, close to Jamestown. An increasing number of land holdings in the area were claimed by English settlers by the late 17th and early 18th century.

Robert Howsing received one of the first land concessions in 1669 in what would become Arlington. Located exactly across from Georgetown on the Virginia side of the Potomac, this parcel covered around 6,000 acres. Nevertheless, the property was sold and then bought by John Alexander for 6,000 pounds of tobacco after going through several other hands. The city of Alexandria, which was formerly a part of the region that is today known as Arlington, gained its name from Alexander.

During these early years, tobacco production was the main cash crop for the Virginia colony, and most of Arlington's land was used for this purpose. But another dark chapter in Arlington's history—the institution of slavery—was brought about by the labor-intensive nature of tobacco production. The socioeconomic structure of the region was further complicated by the forced labor of Africans who were enslaved and forced to labor on the plantations. It is impossible to overestimate their lasting influence on Arlington; their contributions, hardships, and tales will be covered in more length in a later chapter.

As the eighteenth century progressed, the political atmosphere grew more volatile. The early stirrings of revolutionary feeling were caused by the discontent that many of the area's residents were experiencing under British control. Because of its close proximity to both the powerful city of Philadelphia and the colonial seat of Williamsburg, Arlington was not isolated from the larger ideological changes occurring throughout the American colonies. As a young man, George Washington inspected land in Arlington and went on to become one of the most memorable personalities of the Revolutionary Era. Eventually, he acquired a nearby plantation, which he developed into a component of his Mount Vernon estate.

In 1775, the Revolutionary War broke out, placing the present-day Arlington region at a strategic location. Among the ranks of those who battled for American independence were men from the area. During the struggle, Alexandria developed into a major port that supplied tobacco and other goods needed to fund the revolution. Arlington did not see any significant conflicts, but the sounds of neighboring cannon and musket fire echoed across the hills and valleys, serving as a daily reminder of the high stakes in the fight for independence and self-determination.

The area west of the Potomac was seen to be a potential location for the capital of the newly formed country after the war. Even though the farms and wetlands that would eventually become Washington, D.C. eventually took first place, Arlington, which later donated property for the federal city's construction, was affected long-term by the decision.

Arlington's early residents had a lasting impression on the area. From a collection of aboriginal settlements and wild forests, they turned it into a portion of a brand-new country united by principles but tarnished by the sins of enslavement and expropriation. It's critical to acknowledge these early people as complicated people who, for better or worse, contributed to the development of Arlington as we know it today rather than as binary heroes or villains. We will discover, as we delve more into the later chapters of Arlington's history, how the choices made by these early residents—big and small—created the framework for a neighborhood at the crossroads of some of the most significant periods in American history.

Therefore, keep in mind that these early settlers are still very much a part of the living, evolving Arlington as you pass by structures that reflect architectural forms they would have recognized or drive along streets named for trees they would have known. Their achievements and shortcomings, their hopes and weaknesses, are woven into the very soil, a proof of the complex fabric that is this singularly American tale.

Chapter 3: Arlington in the Colonial Era

Looking through the maze-like archives of Arlington's past, the colonial period is a crucial period when the features of a nascent town start to take shape. Although the foundation was formed by the early settlers, it is during this time that the region experiences revolutionary changes that play a crucial role in the development of Arlington as it is today. The scene is broad, including socioeconomic changes, political upheavals, and the emergence of a growing feeling of regional identity.

What is today known as Arlington was a portion of Fairfax County, which was formed in 1742 by the division of the larger Prince William County, during the colonial era. Named for Thomas Fairfax, the 6th Lord Fairfax of Cameron, Fairfax County was a center of commerce and agriculture. With the brutal institution of slavery serving as both a vital component of the region's economy and a seriously defective foundation of its social structure, tobacco production remained the dominant industry in the area.

But somewhere beyond the humid veil of the Potomac and the tobacco fields, something else was fermenting. After the Enlightenment arrived in Europe, its principles started to seep into Virginia's colonial taverns and salons. Even in Fairfax County, where there is a strong tobacco smell, there were traces of this intellectual awakening, even though Arlington may not have been a center of philosophical discussion like Philadelphia or Boston. Words of liberty, republicanism, and self-governance started to filter through to the local population. These concepts would become increasingly popular in the second half of the 18th century.

Important infrastructure was established during the colonial era, sowing the seeds of community development. Churches began to appear all over the place, frequently functioning as both public meeting places and places of worship. Among the earliest religious establishments in the area, Truro Parish was established in 1732 and had an influence on the area that would become Arlington. Although they were established gradually, schools were also established at the period because the majority of instruction was done privately, at home. As transportation routes—mainly primitive roads and ferries—began to crisscross the region, Arlington became more connected to its neighbors and more easily accessible.

Additionally, Arlington saw the start of the development of its first long-lasting architectural landmarks during this time. A few brick residences and buildings from the late colonial era still intact, providing us with an insight into the practical and aesthetic decisions made during the time, even though the majority of the early timber structures have not survived. Among these is Arlington's oldest house, the Ball-Sellers House, which dates back to about 1750. The modest, timber-frame home, in stark contrast to the opulence of plantation houses, offers insightful insights into the everyday life of common colonists.

Arlington gained significance as colonial tensions between the United States and Great Britain increased toward the conclusion of the colonial era due to its placement near important military and political hubs. A number of its citizens would participate in the Revolutionary War as fighters, providers, or allies. The region's connection to George Washington created an additional historical resonance. Arlington's people and resources were involved in the historic conflict even if the city's soil would not be stained red from Revolutionary War conflicts.

The end of colonialism is marked by a great sense of expectation. A new nation is finally established after an independence declaration, victories, and defeats in war. With the Revolutionary War officially over and the 18th century coming to an end, Arlington found itself on the cusp of an exciting and potentially unpredictable future with the signing of the Treaty of Paris in 1783. Its residents may not have realized it at the time, but their little town would eventually play major, minor, or even pivotal roles in the grand American drama that was about to take place.

Thus, remember the colonial past that gave this area its original layers of significance as you stroll through its contemporary streets and drive over its motorways while taking in its skyline. The accomplishments, setbacks, and struggles of this era continue to reverberate, intricately woven within Arlington, Virginia's multifaceted tapestry. The colonial age is not a closed book but rather a dynamic story whose people and tales live on in the buildings, the landscape, and the unwavering pursuit of liberty and community that characterizes the American experience.

Chapter 4: Important Landmarks and their History

Every building you come across in Arlington's modern environment is more than just brick and mortar; it's a guardian angel watching over the passage of time, and everyone has a story to tell. The sites you see are markers on the historical map that lead us through different periods that have influenced Arlington's future. With the ability to travel through time as simply as you could cross a street today, let's wander through the histories of a few of these iconic locations. Every landmark acts as a center of attention, drawing tales to it in a manner similar to a magnet drawing iron filings and contributing to the development of a palpable, spatial connection to the region's historical fabric.

Maybe start with the Arlington National Cemetery, a name that connotes respect and sacrifice made on behalf of the country. Although the site of the cemetery has been associated with various stories, such as being a portion of Robert E. Lee's plantation or a community for freedmen, it was transformed into a graveyard dedicated to honoring the memory of soldiers who lost their lives defending their nation following the Civil War. It is a monument to the country's collective memory and more than merely a cemetery. The Tomb of the Unknown Soldier, which is manned by guards around-the-clock, 365 days a year, gives this iconic location even more significance as it honors the warriors whose names are lost but who are remembered in addition to the ones whose identities are known.

Let us now examine the Pentagon, which houses the US Department of Defense headquarters. With a total area of almost six million square feet, the enormous building casts a lengthy shadow both physically and figuratively. Not only is its construction an architectural marvel, but it was completed in just 16 months during the early years of World War II and holds a significant place in the annals of global military history. Within its confines, during the Cold War, plans were developed to influence global geopolitical processes. The structure itself tragically became the center of attention following the September 11, 2001 terrorist attacks, highlighting the building's significance as a symbol of US military might.

An additional doorway into the complexity of history is provided by Arlington House, popularly known as the Robert E. Lee Memorial. George Washington Parke Custis, his step-grandson, planned the mansion, which was finished in 1818. It was meant to be a house for the Washington family as well as a memorial to the man. The estate's history took a tragic turn when the Civil War broke out because its resident at the time, Robert E. Lee, decided to join the Confederate cause and resign his commission in the U.S. Army. After that, the estate was taken up by Union forces and turned into the Arlington National Cemetery.

The Marine Corps War Memorial, also referred to as the Iwo Jima Memorial, is another. The monument honors all U.S. Marine Corps members who have died while serving their nation, and it was inspired by Joe Rosenthal's famous image of the flag being raised during the Battle of Iwo Jima. Since its 1954 dedication, it has served as a constant reminder of the costs incurred in preserving democracy and freedom.

Not every landmark in Arlington is large or has a broad national significance. Located in Arlington, the oldest structure, the Ball-Sellers House, captures the simpler side of life in the eighteenth century. The Long Branch Nature Center is another example of the region's dedication to environmental education and preservation; it serves as a kind of symbol for how modernity and history may coexist in a sustainable manner.

Certain landmarks are clearly significant historically, but others are significant because they enhance everyday living and foster community togetherness. Schools, parks, and even business buildings can become landmarks in and of themselves since they serve as the backdrop for the drama that is Arlington's daily existence. A school may appear to be just a structure, but generations of Arlingtonians have been educated there for the real world, making it an integral part of the community's history on par with any leader's mansion or war memorial.

Arlington's landmarks function as individual volumes in a library as well as chapters in a book. Although each has a unique story to tell, taken as a whole, they tell a complete story that both answers questions about the past and addresses the needs and goals of the present. Ultimately, they are dynamic, living pieces of a community's past that invite each of us to join them in telling their continuing tale, rather than merely being static objects to be observed and captured on camera.

Chapter 5: Arlington during the American Revolution

Through the pages of Arlington's history, we come to a critical moment, when the fledgling colonies were ablaze with revolutionary zeal. Fairfax County's Arlington was engulfed in the whirlwind of events that would transform the continent amid screams for independence and the deafening din of muskets and cannons. Peeling back the layers of mythology and examining the land and its people, their loyalties and tensions, and the local incidents that reflected the greater ideological battle unfolding across the thirteen colonies is necessary to comprehend Arlington's significance during the American Revolution.

The area that would become Arlington was mostly agricultural during the Revolutionary War, consisting of farms and huge estates. The area held some strategic significance due to its close proximity to important areas such as Alexandria and the Potomac River. However, the people who inhabited the land also contributed to the complexity of Arlington's position throughout this time. While some of the most well-known families in the region were fervently committed to revolution, others were devoted to the Crown as Loyalists. This dualism produced a tense atmosphere where people were wary of one another and there was a chance that disagreements over ideologies would blow up in flames.

An explanation of Arlington's revolutionary past would be incomplete if it did not include a mention of the magnificent stone building known as Carlyle House in Alexandria, which was the headquarters of British General Edward Braddock. The home was the scene of important military planning and political negotiations, highlighting the region's participation in the greater British war effort prior to the revolutionaries' conflagration spreading throughout the colonies. Young George Washington accompanied Braddock on his disastrous mission against the French in 1755, which laid the groundwork for the types of military operations the region would see again a few decades later.

Throughout the war, there were frequent conflicts along the Potomac River. In addition to acting as a natural barrier, it was an important trade route that both American and British armies fought for control. Along the Potomac, there were many battles and naval encounters as both sides realized that commanding the river would provide them with strategic and tactical benefits. The seas that surrounded Arlington turned into a battlefield as a result, with forces loyalist and patriot battling for supremacy.

What about the average people, the homemakers, blacksmiths, and farmers whose names may never have appeared in history books? The war was a time of hardship and uncertainty for these people. Regardless of their intellectual commitment to the cause of independence, the conflict created a continual threat of violence, hindered trade, and reduced resource availability. Many found their lands and resources taken over for the war effort, or they were forced to give quarter to the armed forces. The elderly, women, and children took up the majority of the family's financial responsibilities while the males were away fighting. Not only was war something you heard in the town square or read about in the papers, but it was a daily reality that came calling for both big and small sacrifices.

Another significant effect of the war was that it sparked social changes that persisted for years to come. The ideals of liberty and equality were spoken to the enslaved people in the region, and they were not unheard. Slavery in the region did not immediately vanish as a result of the revolution, but the ideological foundation for opposing the system had been established. Discussions concerning freedom invariably gave rise to inquiries concerning the contradiction of defending freedom while denying it to those who are oppressed.

Like most of the colonies, Arlington was radically changed after the revolution. As loyalist estates were seized and dispersed, landholdings changed. The revolutionary ideas that had been battled for started to take shape in the form of new laws and mechanisms of governance. With the birth of a new country, a new chapter in Arlington's history could be written.

As we come to the end of the chapter on Arlington during the American Revolution, it is evident that the region was an active participant in the events of the day, a minor but important player on the bigger revolutionary stage, rather than only a passive backdrop. The ideas that now serve as the country's compass, the landmarks, and the descendants of the families who experienced those revolutionary periods all bear witness to the echoes of those turbulent days. Let us remember the sacrifices, discussions, and everyday hardships that marked this pivotal period as we walk throughout Arlington's territory. They are an essential component of the intricate heritage that Arlington—and America—will carry forward for generations to come.

Chapter 6: Local Heroes and Events of Note

Through the process of unraveling Arlington's historical fabric, the details of specific lives and isolated incidents become more apparent. Though they may not be as well-known as the great narratives of American history, these local heroes and notable incidents are the vivid details that lend depth and richness to the broader story. Men and women who have made remarkable life achievements, interesting eccentricities, and unshakable devotion to their community and country have called Arlington home. This chapter shines a light on these lesser-known but no less worthy individuals and events, each of which is a story jewel just waiting to be unearthed.

A discussion of local heroes would be incomplete without mentioning E. Leslie Hammack, a notable individual from the early 1900s. A devoted supporter of learning and civic involvement, Hammack played a key role in the establishment of Arlington's first public library. His idea was to create a location where all locals, regardless of age, could benefit from the riches of human knowledge, improving the neighborhood as a whole. Thanks in great part to Hammack's efforts, the library—which was once simply a single room within the local high school—grew to become a cultural cornerstone. In addition, he was a multiterm member of the Arlington County School Board, where he implemented progressive policies that enhanced learning opportunities for all kids.

Dr. Phoebe Hall Knipling is another noteworthy person. She was the first female high school science supervisor in Arlington Public Schools. She wasn't satisfied with just teaching in a classroom, so she spearheaded the creation of the 225-acre outdoor learning center known as the Outdoor Lab in Fauquier County, Virginia. Dr. Knipling developed a tool that Arlington Public Schools still utilize today because she felt that exposure to outdoors was fundamental to a well-rounded education.

Additionally, events that occurred locally on Arlington's soil have resonance with larger themes in American history. A notable example is the desegregation of Stratford Junior High School in 1959. Michael Jones, Gloria Thompson, Ronald Deskins, and Lance Newman were the four African-American students who showed bravery during the incident, which was a part of the greater campaign against racial segregation. As the first in the Commonwealth of Virginia to integrate a public school, these young heroes established a precedent and turned became icons for the broader civil rights movement. Their legacy is ingrained in Arlington's identity for all time, and their bravery in the face of institutional and social opposition exemplified the very ideas upon which the country was established.

Not every hero donned a cape, or even just a suit and tie. Regular people have also been instrumental in this effort. One example is the local conservation groups' members, who have battled to protect Arlington's green spaces against the unrelenting advance of urban expansion. Potomac Overlook Regional Park's history provides evidence of these endeavors. In the 1960s, a group of committed locals and environmentalists banded together to stop the site from being sold to developers, guaranteeing that the park would continue to be a haven for both animals and people looking for a break from the city.

Although American culture tends to place a lot of importance on military heroes, Arlington also has its fair share of heroes in the military, most notably those buried in Arlington National Cemetery. The cemetery serves as hallowed ground where the sacrifices of many for the welfare of the nation are respectfully commemorated. Notable personalities like General John J. Pershing are interred there, as is the

Tomb of the Unknown Soldier, which honors unidentified U.S. service personnel.

Examining these noteworthy local figures and events reveals a colorful tapestry of human effort, adversity, and success. These tales are the threads that bind Arlington's past together, giving it a life and significance that still have resonance in our times. Educators, activists, soldiers, and regular people have all added to the continuous story of Arlington, which is entwined with the greater story of the American experience in a dance of inspiration and impact.

Chapter 7: Post-Revolution Changes and Development

Arlington stood on the cusp of a new era as the smoke from the American Revolution dissipated. Now, the fledgling republic was busy creating its institutions, laws, and identity; local effects were also felt from this metamorphosis. Less than had the last lines of the Revolutionary War been written when Arlington began to undergo a series of upheavals and events that would determine its course for many years to come.

Arlington, which was formerly a part of Fairfax County before being retroceded to become Alexandria County and subsequently Arlington County, saw a spike in population in the years immediately following the revolution. Many different types of people were drawn to the newly formed United States by the prospect of opportunity, ranging from aspirational business owners to proficient artisans. The rural setting started to give way to a more intricate, diverse community with a booming business sector. Shops, hotels, and artisan workshops began to appear all over the place, transforming the area into a bustling marketplace where commodities and ideas were freely traded.

Arlington saw a radical transformation in the early 19th century as a result of the growth of transportation networks. For example, the Aqueduct Bridge made it simpler to travel from Arlington to Washington, which had been designated as the nation's capital in 1790. Arlington gained strategic significance that it had not previously experienced due to its close proximity to the center of national power. After the bridge was finished in 1843, traffic accelerated, resulting in more wealth and securing Arlington's position as a major entry point to the capital.

The social fabric of Arlington was likewise impacted by post-revolutionary developments. Arlington, like a large portion of Virginia, was a slaveholding community, and as time went on, the topic of slavery grew more divisive. Some inhabitants remained steadfast in their belief that slavery was fundamental to their way of life, while others started to doubt the ethics and viability of a slave-based economy. The decades preceding the Civil War brought this division to light. Once-unifying organizations, churches were now divided on the issue of slavery, which resulted in splits and the creation of new denominations.

The national tension was reflected in the intellectual struggle over slavery, which also predicted the profound transformations Arlington would undergo during the Civil War—a topic we will address in a later chapter. However, Arlington was going through various kinds of societal change even prior to the Civil War. New educational institutions were established, and civic associations began to spring up, indicating a community interested in improving itself and holding public discussions.

Arlington began to notice the effects of technical improvements around the middle of the 19th century. Arlington was more closely linked to the national and even international grids with the advent of the telegraph and then the train. Operating from the 1840s to the Civil War, the Alexandria Canal was an important economic channel that connected Arlington to Georgetown and made it easier to move commodities including coal, grain, and flour.

Visible changes were also made to Arlington's landscape. Throughout the course of the 18th century, what was essentially farmland gave way to a patchwork of public spaces, business centers, and residential neighborhoods. A portion of the land that had been used for farming was sold to fund construction. Public buildings began to appear, acting as tangible representations of a community that was expanding in both size and complexity.

During this post-Revolutionary era of transformation and growth, ideas and reality collided and combined to create something entirely new. What had once been a boiling pot of revolutionary zeal was now an experiment in contradictions and American ideals. Arlington was endowed with a persistent spirit of change throughout these dynamic years, one that would carry it through the numerous obstacles and victories that were ahead of it. The town would continue to have its own unique identity throughout, reflecting the larger problems, successes, and aspirations of the country.

Chapter 8: Industry and Infrastructure Growth

With the start of the 19th century, industry began to spread southward in America as the northern states were being overtaken by it. Arlington was hardly an exception to this period of profound change. Civil War devastation was still being felt in the city, but the groundwork for future industrial and infrastructural development was being laid. What had been essentially an agrarian setting was about to undergo a dramatic transformation into a more intricately linked community that would be inextricably linked to the country's larger economic currents.

The industrial revolution was sparked by the railroad's introduction in the late 1800s. Arlington had long benefited geographically from its closeness to the nation's capital, but now that train tracks had been installed, it was immediately connected to resources and markets across the country. These train connections made Arlington a hub for innovation and trade by carrying not just commodities but also people, ideas, and opportunities. With the area's rich economic soil, industries including textiles, woodworking, and eventually automobile assembly started to flourish.

But the path to industrial expansion was not an easy one. It presented a unique set of difficulties, chief among them being the labor issue. The labor market saw a great deal of volatility following the Civil War and the emancipation of the enslaved. Freed from institutional discrimination, African Americans moved in pursuit of better prospects. Despite the persistent social injustices that beset them, they were vital to the developing industries. Moreover, immigrants started to arrive in Arlington, bringing a variety of skills that contributed to the city's industrial development.

The noteworthy advancements in infrastructure were another indication of the drive towards contemporary life. The days of crude bridges and dirt trails defining the community's transportation infrastructure were long gone. Better waterways, stronger bridges, and paved roads replaced them; these were funded by both public and private sources of funding. As electricity started to light up the cities around the country, Arlington too started to wean itself off of gas and oil lamps. In the late 19th and early 20th centuries, the community became electrified, which marked a significant step towards modern living and had an impact on everything from factory production to household life.

However, infrastructure encompassed more than just the physical construction of rail and roads; it also involved the development of social and educational institutions. Public halls, schools, and libraries started to appear all around Arlington. The creation of these organizations was a reflection of a rising realization that the intellectual and social well-being of the community's residents had as much importance as the community's industrial power in determining its destiny.

Increased trade and commerce resulted from the emergence of neighborhood markets and stores. Trading days that had previously been irregular turned into busy daily events, which were further enhanced by the expansion of banking institutions. Aspiring entrepreneurs were able to launch new businesses thanks to loans from banks and financial institutions, which sparked the economic cycle.

Thus, Arlington looked very different at the turn of the 20th century than it had in the past. The neighborhood was undergoing a significant metamorphosis with the goal of capitalizing on the immense opportunities presented by industrialization. However, this historical period also brought up difficult issues of environmental responsibility, fair growth, and social justice, the consequences of which can still be heard today as you walk through Arlington's historical corridors.

Arlington's transformation from a predominantly agricultural hamlet to a thriving industrial center had a significant impact on all facets of community life. It was a time of remarkable progress and thought-provoking social issues—a dichotomy that would define Arlington for many years to come. With this, the community was ready to enter the twentieth century, a century that would bring about unthinkable change, and one in which Arlington would play a leading role. The lattice of ever-expanding infrastructure and the pulsing rhythm of industry were portents of an exciting but uncertain future.

Chapter 9: Arlington During the Civil War

In the middle of the 19th century, the threat of civil war hovered over the United States, eventually casting a fog on Arlington as well. Located in Virginia, a state steeped in the problems that gave rise to the Civil War, Arlington emerged as a pivotal battleground in this historic conflict. If you could turn back time and explore Arlington, Virginia in the 1860s, you would find a society that has been drastically altered by the demands of war. The peaceful cadences of rural existence vanished, replaced by the unceasing patter of marching boots, the churning wheels of artillery, and the fearful tones of a populace engulfed in a massive upheaval.

Arlington was a strategic asset that both sides desired due to its close proximity to Washington, D.C. Arlington was caught up in a tense military occupation as Union and Confederate forces fought for control of important military positions. In order to safeguard the nation's capital, Union forces moved quickly to take possession of Arlington when Virginia formally withdrew from the Union in April 1861. Overnight, military outposts appeared, converting the peaceful terrain into a fortified stronghold. The construction of Fort Ethan Allen and Fort Myer, which both acted as vital outposts for Union forces during the fight, is the most noteworthy of them.

However, Arlington was more than just a strategically important location; it was a neighborhood severely impacted by the political divisions that split the country. Families became split up because some members choose to join the Confederate army while others supported the Union. Many local citizens left as Union forces became noticeable, leaving behind homes and lands that the Union government would later seize. A portion of these lands were transformed into Freedmen's villages, providing newly freed African Americans with a place to live.

In Arlington, the human drama of the Civil War was evident. In order to care for the injured, hospitals were built; the most well-known of them is the Arlington House, which Union forces took early in the conflict. After being transformed into a hospital, it witnessed a constant stream of soldiers with illnesses and war wounds, an excruciating reminder of the high human cost the conflict exacted. This house has its own terrible meaning, acting as a microcosm of a divided country. It had originally been the home of Confederate Army General Robert E. Lee.

It's critical to keep in mind that the Civil War involved a conflict between beliefs as much as forces. Arlington was not an exception to the state of Virginia's pervasive societal fabric of slavery. Slavery started to disintegrate in the town as Union soldiers seized power and the Emancipation Proclamation went into force. Many enslaved individuals took advantage of the chance to gain their freedom and enlisted in the Union army as workers, soldiers, or spies. To many, the war represented a fight for emancipation and the beginning of a long road toward civil rights, one that would eventually prove to be far from finished.

When we take a broader view of Arlington during the Civil War, we see a rich, multidimensional tableau. Here was a community that was changing at a faster rate than before, its social fabric being ripped and reconstructed under the intense strain of a country at war. Arlington was put to the test by the experience of war, which also acted as a catalyst, making it face the most difficult moral and social concerns of the day.

After the war ended in 1865, Arlington had undergone permanent change. Its topography was characterized by military engagement scars, cemeteries, and forts. Its population had also experienced a profound change, both in terms of quantity and awareness. Arlington stood on the cusp of a new age, humbled yet hopeful, as the Reconstruction era began. The war was over, but the battle to define Arlington's post-war identity had only just begun. It was the end of one chapter, but it was also the beginning of another, a complicated web of conflict, evolution, and change that would continue to mold Arlington for many more.

Chapter 10: Reconstruction and its Impact

For Arlington, Virginia, as it was for the South and the country at large, reconstruction was a trial by fire. After the Civil War, Arlington had to tackle the enormous challenge of reconstructing not only its physical infrastructure but also its social organization. Old economic systems had collapsed, societal hierarchies had become unstable, and most significantly, a sizable segment of the African American population had been freed as a result of the conflict. Thus, Arlington battled with existential problems about identity, governance, and social equality during the Reconstruction era, which was a time of both opportunity and uncertainty.

The position of Arlington's African American population changed, and this was the most noticeable and rapid alteration. Enslaved persons were freed after the Civil War ended and the Thirteenth Amendment was ratified. Communities such as Freedmen's Village offered recently freed Black citizens a chance at self-governance and community development. Freedmen's Village, built on the site of Confederate General Robert E. Lee's estate, served as a practical and symbolic contrast to Arlington's antebellum heritage. In and around the village, shops, schools, and churches sprang up, serving as fertile ground for the future social and economic development of the African American population. However, draconian "Black Codes" and subsequent Jim Crow laws that attempted to impose racial segregation and second-class citizenship blocked the promise of full social and political inclusion for Black Americans.

Economic and social transformations were mutually reinforcing. A substantial portion of the pre-war economy was built on an agrarian model that relied on slave labor. This economic system has to be adjusted in light of the abolition of slavery. Although agriculture continued to be a significant industry, particularly in the county's more rural parts, attention increasingly shifted toward more diverse sources of income. Services, light manufacturing, and retail establishments started to penetrate Arlington's economy. Large-scale public works initiatives were also undertaken during the Reconstruction era with the goal of repairing and enhancing public buildings, roads, and bridges, creating jobs and laying the groundwork for future economic growth.

Changes in politics were as important. Virginia was under military occupation during Reconstruction, and the state's approval of the Reconstruction Acts was a requirement for Virginia's readmission into the Union. As a result, Virginia's political and legal system was revised. Black men were granted the right to vote, which resulted in their election to a number of public seats. However, racist policies would later restrict their political enfranchisement. Like other Southern communities, Arlington had to adjust to a new, supposedly more democratic and egalitarian form of government while navigating these changes in the political power landscape.

Progress in education was another noteworthy feature of this era. During Reconstruction, public education was established in Virginia, although segregated classrooms were the norm. Despite receiving distinct and frequently unequal resources, Black schools developed as hubs of ambition and community. The social and economic standing of the Black community as a whole, as well as that of their students, was greatly improved by the teachers in these institutions, many of whom were also community leaders.

However, it is imperative to recognize that Reconstruction was as much a period of development as it was of unmet expectations. The early efforts toward social justice and racial equality encountered strong opposition, which led to the creation of laws with limiting provisions and the rise of groups like the Ku Klux Klan that were dedicated to upholding white supremacy. Arlington was deeply impacted by this complex history, which had a lasting impact that extended well into the 20th century and influenced the Civil Rights Movement and other movements.

When the Reconstruction era came to an official conclusion in 1877, Arlington had seen a period of transformation that left a mixed legacy. Although it created the groundwork for later advances in economic and civil rights, it also left unresolved conflicts and tensions that would trouble the community for many years to come. Gaining an understanding of Reconstruction in Arlington is essential to understanding the complex web of social, political, and economic strands that have subsequently come together to form this diverse American community's current identity.

Chapter 11: Arlington in the Gilded Age

The Gilded Age began in the United States when the country's Civil War wounds started to heal and the hardships of Reconstruction became less prominent. The late 19th and early 20th centuries saw a fast urbanization and industrialization of society, as well as the accumulation of unparalleled wealth by a small elite. The era's paradox was summed up by Mark Twain's term "Gilded Age," which described a glittering exterior of affluence and advancement that concealed pervasive social and economic inequality.

Even though the industrial areas and the ascent of tycoons like Andrew Carnegie and John D. Rockefeller provided the most striking examples of the Gilded Age, other locations, such as Arlington, Virginia, were also greatly impacted. Railroads expanded during this time, facilitating a more seamless connection between Arlington and the larger US economy. The Washington and Old Dominion Railroad, which traveled through what is now Arlington, was a major factor in the area's opening to urban influences and economic growth from Washington, D.C.

During this time, Arlington's agricultural economy started to change as a result of the railroad's bigger market forces and the impending industrialization. With the ease with which goods could now be moved to profitable urban markets, traditional, more self-contained agricultural practices started to give way to dairy farming and market gardening. During this time, new farming equipment and techniques were also introduced, which increased farming productivity but also signaled the beginning of a long-term trend that would see agriculture lose economic significance in Arlington.

Arlington also embodied the Gilded Age ideals of individual initiative and material advancement through architecture. Many of Arlington's historic homes, which exhibit the ornate embellishment and ostentation that defined the era's architecture, were built during this time. There was an increase in the number of Queen Anne and Victorian-style mansions with elaborate woodwork, large porches, and often ornamental towers.

But not everyone believed in the promises of prosperity and advancement made during this time. The Gilded Age brought with it increasing racial segregation and a lack of economic opportunity for African Americans in Arlington. The emergence of Jim Crow laws and institutionalized discrimination fostered an atmosphere of disenfranchisement, despite the fact that the abolition of slavery and the Reconstruction era had provided a glimpse of possible social transformation. After being dissolved in the late 19th century as a government camp for freed slaves during the Civil War, Freedman's Village's residents were forced to find new homes and possibilities in a society where racial barriers were becoming more and more prevalent.

In Arlington, women were also subject to the limitations of the day; they were primarily restricted to the home and were not granted many of the economic and legal privileges enjoyed by males. But the seeds of change were being planted for the future. Across the country, the suffrage movement was gaining steam, and Arlington women were among those who started campaigning, organizing, and debating for the right to vote.

In conclusion, Arlington throughout the Gilded Age served as a microcosm for the more significant changes occurring across the nation. At the same time, there was progress and paradox. Larger forces of industrialization, urbanization, and social change profoundly altered Arlington's economy, scenery, and society. Arlington was forever changed at this time, as new architectural wonders and railroads cut through peaceful countryside, establishing the groundwork for

Arlington to grow into the thriving metropolis it would become in the 20th century. However, the battles and societal divides that characterized the time also left a legacy of their own, one that would take on new shapes and give rise to new conflicts in the decades that followed.

Chapter 12: The Rise of Technology and its Effects

With the 20th century bringing with it an overwhelming array of technological innovations, Arlington, Virginia, was at the center of this revolutionary era. Arlington's closeness to Washington, D.C., growing infrastructure, and educated population made it a desirable destination for government agencies and technology-related businesses. This had a significant impact on the cultural and economic fabric of the region.

Arlington's technical boom can be attributed to the post-World War II period, when the US concentrated on scientific and technological advancement to maintain its military might and economic prosperity. The city profited from this concentration as the federal government increased its investment in these areas, housing a variety of governmental organizations and for-profit businesses developing cutting-edge technologies. During this time, Arlington started to host other Department of Defense functions as well as installations like the Pentagon. A fertile ground for invention and research was formed by the infusion of military and technological intelligence work, which forged a cooperative relationship with nearby educational institutions.

But the explosion of technology was not restricted to uses in the military. As the personal computer revolution swept the country in the 1980s and 1990s, Arlington witnessed a boom in IT companies and information technology services. The city became a center for internet-based services, data analytics, and software development. Arlington had a boom in its economy as a result of the entry of IT companies, which also created high-paying jobs that drew in talented laborers from all over the nation.

The development of technology physically changed the city's topography. As more tech businesses chose Arlington as their headquarters, it became clear that they needed cutting-edge infrastructure. Sleek, contemporary structures that housed data centers, labs, and state-of-the-art production facilities replaced older structures. During this time, the Metro system was expanded into Arlington in order to accommodate the growing commute needs of thousands of computer professionals.

The local school system was significantly impacted by the technology revolution as well. Acknowledging the need to equip students for a work market that is changing quickly, educational institutions started including computer science and programming into their curricula. Due to the overwhelming need for STEM (Science, Technology, Engineering, and Math) education, IT corporations and educational institutions have partnered for mutual benefit. By obtaining funding and endowments from both public and private tech companies, nearby colleges and universities including Marymount University and George Mason University increased their capacity for doing tech-related research and developing tech-related courses.

But there were drawbacks to this technological rebirth as well. Arguments concerning cheap housing and neighborhood gentrification arose as a result of the flood of highly compensated IT workers, which raised living standards and property values. A more ephemeral population that was less steeped in the history and culture of the place was another result of the shifting demography. The development of technology also led to more surveillance and concerns about data privacy.

The technology industry also had to deal with inclusion and diversity challenges. Even while the industry brought enormous riches and opportunity, not every area of Arlington's population benefited equally from them. Conversations concerning the presence of women and minorities in tech enterprises merged with the city's larger social equity conversation. These discussions were important but frequently difficult steps in creating a community that is more inclusive.

Regarding civic government, technology has opened up new avenues for improving openness and citizen participation. In an effort to create a more educated and engaged community, the local government implemented digital platforms for public records, outreach, and service delivery.

The rise of technology in Arlington is a multifaceted story with social, cultural, and ethical undertones in addition to being a story of economic success. Capturing the essence of modern Arlington, a city at the nexus of history and modernity, wrestling with the opportunities and challenges that come with being a key role in the age of technology, requires an understanding of this shift.

Chapter 13: Arlington during WWI and WWII

Like the rest of the country, Arlington would undergo irreversible upheaval as a result of events taking place thousands of miles away when the world entered the chaos of World War I in 1914. Even though the United States didn't officially enter the war until 1917, Arlington was significantly impacted by the militarization wave that preceded it. Originally constructed as a fortification during the Civil War, Fort Myer has since evolved into a thriving military installation that trains cavalry regiments and even acts as a test site for cutting-edge military technology like the military airplane. In fact, the first military aviation fatality would happen at Fort Myer in 1908, bringing with it the unsettling arrival of a technology that would revolutionize warfare in the 20th century.

However, the Second World War was the catalyst for Arlington's significant transformation into its current configuration. Arlington was in the center of the storm as the US gathered economic and military forces for an unprecedented worldwide conflict. The urgent, vast militarization that was taking place was physically manifested in 1941–1942 with the construction of the Pentagon. The Pentagon, which was constructed in a just 16 months, was an impressive feat of technical and logistical skill and at the time the largest office structure in the world. When it was established, the military's center of gravity was moved near Arlington, giving the quickly growing defense organization a focal point.

Arlington would house not only military sites but also intelligence offices and research and development activities due to its close proximity to the nation's capital. Due to the influx of thousands of engineers, spies, and service members drawn to Arlington by these organizations, the city saw a significant increase in population as well as the development of public housing and other amenities. It was at this time that the neighborhoods we now recognize as being uniquely Arlington, like as Ballston, Crystal City, and Rosslyn, started to take development, home to military families and government employees.

Additionally, the war era sparked societal shifts that would have a long-term impact on the neighborhood. In many fields of work, barriers based on race and gender have loosened as a result of the pressing need for labor. Although they frequently experienced prejudice and segregation, women and African Americans were able to find career possibilities in new federal positions. Freedman's Village, a government-established colony for freed slaves during the Civil War that lasted into the 20th century, was built as a result of the war effort's urgency. Within the larger framework of the civil rights movement, the experiences of the war years would be a crucial background against which the post-war racial equality movements would build.

Women were also quite important at this time. When males were sent to serve overseas, women filled positions that had previously been off-limits to them, such as secretarial work, physically taxing employment in industries, and even auxiliary military duty. These deeply personal and collective experiences would subsequently challenge traditional gender roles and expectations and help give rise to the women's rights movement.

Arlington saw a scholarly and cultural boom during the war years. A melting pot of ideas and cultures was produced by the infusion of a wide range of people, including scientists, foreign diplomats, spies, codebreakers, and troops from all across the nation. The later rise of Arlington as a center of creativity and technology was also partly fueled by the necessity for secrecy and the presence of a sizable, highly educated workforce.

Arlington was a semi-rural suburb when the Second World War ended, but it was soon a thriving metropolis that was intertwined into the intricate web of international political, military, and economic systems. Aside from being permanently altered, the human landscape of Arlington was also complicated, rich, and shaped by the various experiences of migration, social transformation, and conflict. Arlington, which had witnessed the profound upheavals of the 20th century and would continue to change in the intricate interaction of local and global forces, was a place fundamentally entwined with the larger currents of American and world history when it emerged from the crucible of the World Wars.

Chapter 14: Military Bases and Economics During WWII

Despite early efforts to remain neutral, the United States found itself drawn into the global battle as the storm clouds of World War II gathered over Europe and Asia. The country needed to significantly expand its military infrastructure, and Arlington, Virginia, was going to be a key component of this endeavor. It was a strategically important location for the expanding American military-industrial complex because of its close proximity to Washington, D.C. The Pentagon's construction, which began in 1941 and was astonishingly completed in just 16 months, is arguably the most iconic image of this era. The Pentagon's architecture, a massive five-sided concrete structure, came to symbolize the enormous logistical and organizational project that the U.S. military would oversee during World War II.

The Pentagon's construction in Arlington was revolutionary in a number of respects. In terms of employment, it gave thousands of locals jobs both during construction and throughout continuous operations. Retail, services, and home building were among the various economic activities in Arlington that were boosted by the Pentagon's presence. The county saw a sharp increase in real estate development, leading to the creation of new communities like Arlington Forest and Fairlington, which were intended to house the inflow of both military and civilian employees. These advancements also catalyzed changes in the infrastructure of transportation. In response to the increased demand for transportation, public transportation services were extended, new highways were built, and existing roads were widened.

Arlington was shaped by military installations other than the Pentagon during this time. An already-existing military station from the Civil War era, Fort Myer underwent major expansion to serve as the center of operations for the Signal Corps. It performed several functions, such as acting as a training and coordination center and a location for military communications technology tests. Radar technology and cryptography systems, among other cutting-edge military technological advancements, were tested on Fort Myer premises.

Numerous societal changes in Arlington were also brought about by the presence of these military sites. The county had a surge in newcomers, which broadened the county's demographic base. Arlington became home to a diverse range of regional cultures, religious traditions, and political beliefs brought by soldiers and civilian people from across the nation. But the war effort also revealed gender and racial inequities. Although African Americans were able to find employment in the rapidly growing defense industry, they were frequently assigned to lower-paying positions and faced racial discrimination. The military was still operating under segregation. However, women discovered new career paths in technical and administrative positions in both the expanding private sector that aided in the war effort and military facilities like the Pentagon.

The mobilization during the war had an impact on the environment as well. Arlington's natural environment experienced changes, not necessarily in a positive way. Loss of green spaces resulted from wartime construction initiatives involving new roads and buildings. Furthermore, the heightened activity and population density exert pressure on regional resources, encompassing waste management and water supply.

There is no denying that Arlington's military installations during World War II had a significant positive economic impact. The bases contributed to the local economy's diversification and strengthening, resulting in a more robust and complex framework that laid the groundwork for success after the war. Nevertheless, there were difficulties and inconsistencies with this expansion. This military buildup brought about a wide range of complicated and long-lasting social and environmental changes, affecting issues of race, gender, and community identity that would continue to develop in the decades that followed. Thus, the story of Arlington during World War II is one of conflict and change, a crucial part of a larger story of how this community has negotiated its place in American history.

Chapter 15: Arlington in the Civil Rights Era

Following the World War II victory elation and the post-war economic boom, Arlington became involved in a web of racial and social conflicts that were a component of the larger Civil Rights Movement that was sweeping the nation. Arlington was a vital front in the fight for racial equality and integration, although not receiving the same attention as Birmingham or Montgomery in the annals of civil rights history. Arlington's actions and court battles often had an impact far beyond its county boundaries because of its close proximity to the nation's capital, which attracted the attention of Washington, D.C. policymakers.

Education was one of the first and most important battlegrounds. Virginia state law firmly supported the practice of racial segregation in Arlington Public Schools. But advocates in Arlington saw a chance to overturn the existing quo following the 1954 Supreme Court ruling in Brown v. Board of Education, which ruled that segregated schools were unconstitutional. Leading organizations that offered organizational and legal support were those such as the National Association for the Advancement of Colored People (NAACP). In 1959, Stratford Junior High School became the first public school in Virginia to admit African American pupils, thereby desegregating the state after years of court disputes and public outcry.

In Arlington, desegregation was not just a legal fight but also a social conflict affecting many areas of public life, such as housing and employment. African Americans had a rise in community activity during this time, driven by their demands for equal opportunities in public places and jobs, supported by the Civil Rights Act of 1964 and the Voting Rights Act of 1965. Simultaneously, the Women's

Liberation movement gathered momentum, forming intricate and fascinating intersections with the drive for racial equality.

Notable among them was the nonpartisan political group known as "Arlingtonians for a Better County" (ABC), which aimed to end racial discrimination in general and housing discrimination in particular. The ABC quietly shaped the political climate in the area by endorsing candidates who promoted integration, open housing, and educational reform. The sit-ins and protests in neighborhood eateries and public areas also raised public awareness of the problem of segregation and its importance, which increased pressure on local government to end discriminatory policies.

The discussions surrounding civil rights were even more heated during the Vietnam War era, as concerns about domestic equality grew more at odds with the story of battling for freedom overseas. Civil rights and anti-war protests frequently blended together to create a more intricate web of social movement. Due to its close proximity to the Pentagon, Arlington was an obvious venue for anti-war demonstrations. These gatherings frequently brought together divergent activist groups, expanding the scope and influence of civil rights activity in the county.

But development was neither smooth nor universally embraced. Desegregation efforts were frequently greeted with strong opposition, which occasionally took the form of "white flight" from public schools or local hostility to open housing proposals. Furthermore, not everyone benefited equally from the era's civil rights gains. Economic hurdles frequently remained in place even after legal barriers were removed, which helped minority populations continue to experience cycles of poverty and disadvantage.

During the Civil Rights era, Arlington is a microcosm of the larger American fight for social justice during this turbulent time. The court cases, social demonstrations, and neighborhood action that took place in the county served as a metaphor for the broader national conversation about democracy, equality, and racism. The fight for civil rights in Arlington was a diverse endeavor that drew from and contributed to the larger currents of social and political change sweeping across the country, from schoolhouses to courthouses, from neighborhood eateries to apartment complexes. Understanding Arlington's past, then, will help one better understand how America dealt with some of the most important and complicated social concerns of the 20th century.

Chapter 16: Other Notable Social Movements in Arlington

Beyond the profound changes brought about by the Civil Rights movement, Arlington has served as a hub for a number of other social movements that have had a noticeable and unnoticed influence on the city's political, social, and cultural environments. Arlington, being near Washington, D.C., has long placed it in a unique position to be both a concentrated location where local issues attain national relevance and a part of broader currents of national debate.

The environmental movement was one such movement that became popular in the late 1960s and early 1970s. Organized community clean-ups, educational fairs, and environmental lobbying were all part of Arlington's 1970 Earth Day celebrations, a practice that has continued and changed over time. As environmental awareness grew, tangible policy reforms were also brought about, such as the 1979 founding of the Arlington Department of Environmental Services, which is in charge of managing natural resources and preparing for sustainability. Arlington has a strong environmental ethic even now, as seen by its efforts in sustainable urban design and the utilization of renewable energy sources in county facilities.

Another important movement in Arlington emerged in the 1980s and 1990s as a result of the AIDS crisis, spearheaded by a group of LGBTQ activists and healthcare advocates. The LGBTQ community gained more prominence as a result of the mobilization surrounding this issue, which also sparked important discussions about discrimination, sexual education, and public health. Since opening its doors in Arlington in 1987 to offer HIV/AIDS testing and counseling, the LGBTQ-focused Whitman-Walker Clinic has played a significant role in the community by promoting the rights and health of underprivileged groups.

There has also been a notable Arlington chapter of feminism. Drawing inspiration from the second wave of feminism that emerged in the 1960s and 1970s and finding new life in the third wave that emerged in the 1990s and beyond, Arlington's feminist activists have successfully influenced local policies. These have included advocating for women's health and safety as well as pushing for educational curricula that highlight the contributions made by women to history. Through community initiatives, a number of women's groups and shelters that address issues such as domestic abuse have been established and maintained, creating forums where women's issues might be given priority and addressed.

The labor movement has also found significant traction in Arlington, particularly in light of the city's increasing immigrant population. Better salaries, workers' rights, and decent working conditions have been campaigned for by groups like the Arlington Workers' Rights Coalition, among others, especially in industries like construction where many immigrants find employment. These movements frequently crossed paths with more general efforts for immigration rights, demonstrating the complex and multifaceted character of social activity in the state.

Like many American cities, Arlington had to deal with increased national security concerns and the ensuing impact on civil liberties in the wake of 9/11. These problems were rendered all the more severe by the Pentagon's proximity—the target of one of the 9/11 attacks. Protests against the USA PATRIOT Act and other counterterrorism measures that they saw to be undermining civil liberties were organized by activist groups. This sparked an extensive public discussion about striking a balance between security and freedom, which is still going on today.

In addition, social justice movements such as Black Lives Matter and, more recently, those supporting the rights of Asian Americans and Pacific Islanders (AAPIs) have emerged and grown in the twenty-first century. Even though these movements are on a national or even international scale, they have devoted supporters in Arlington who have planned demonstrations, conducted policy advocacy, and run educational initiatives. As a result, the county's social involvement has been enhanced.

Arlington thus functions as a tiny mirror reflecting the bigger setbacks and victories of numerous social movements that have formed and still shape the United States. It is a particularly fascinating case study of how local, national, and international issues intersect in the activism of a single town because of its distinct geographic position and diversified population. The different social movements that have settled in Arlington are interwoven strands in the larger tapestry of American social history, not isolated occurrences.

Chapter 17: Technological Revolution of the 20th Century to the Millennium

Arlington found itself not just as a bystander but also as an active participant in the global technology revolution that reshaped both the United States and the world as the 20th century gave way to the 21st. Arlington benefited from its close proximity to political authority, military sites, and important educational institutions, all just a short distance from the nation's capital. Because of its advantageous location, the region became a hub for innovation and a refuge for scientists, technocrats, and entrepreneurs who helped to define the new digital era.

The Cold War rivalry and military superiority played a major role in the federal government's role as one of the main forces behind the advancement of technological innovation in the middle of the 20th century. Many technology advancements in Arlington were originally military in character, which is not surprising given the county's close proximity to important governmental institutions like the Pentagon. The foundation for innovations ranging from robots to the internet was created by the Defense Advanced Research Projects Agency (DARPA), which was established in 1958 and had offices in Arlington for a large portion of its existence.

Due to the quick advancements in microprocessor technology, mainframe computers, which were previously the size of vast rooms, began to shrink in the 1960s and 1970s. Businesses based in Arlington or having significant headquarters there started experimenting with data analytics, software development, and information technology—sector areas that would experience rapid expansion in the ensuing decades. These were frequently businesses who had contracts with the government already in place, but they decided to diversify after seeing the writing on the wall.

The personal computer age began in the 1980s, bringing with it a rapid advancement in both hardware and software. Start-ups, or tiny tech-based businesses, began to proliferate in Arlington as they looked to take advantage of this quickly expanding industry. At this point, the Internet began to change from a network used by academics and the government to one that was increasingly open to the public and businesses. DARPA's previous groundbreaking innovation in networking technology discovered unexpected new and wide applications.

The "dot-com" era was well underway by the 1990s. The importance of the Internet had changed from being a luxury to a need, and maximizing and monetizing it had replaced the previous focus on just having a digital presence. The late 1990s and early 2000s dot-com bubble produced some spectacular failures, but it also brought about a necessary correction in the market, reorienting the technology industry toward sustainable development and innovation. Businesses in the telecommunications, software, and cyber-security sectors discovered Arlington to be especially encouraging, with a staff with a high level of expertise and a well-established IT infrastructure.

Then the millennium arrived, bringing with it the age of social media, smart devices, and data analytics. These days, everything revolved around connectedness and the alleged "Internet of Things." Arlington's local government started implementing tech-based solutions for public services, such as public Wi-Fi zones designed to make the Internet accessible to all citizens and traffic control systems that made use of real-time data analytics.

It also placed cybersecurity into striking relief in the post-9/11 environment. Because of its strategic significance, Arlington developed into a center for businesses that specialize in cybersecurity, making it a major participant in both the public and private sectors. This change had societal ramifications in addition to technological ones. Discussions in coffee shops and the corridors of local government offices echoed the general dialogue, which included privacy issues, queries about surveillance, and worries about data integrity.

Beyond merely a shift in the year, the 20th and 21st centuries marked a revolutionary era that fundamentally altered the ways in which we work, live, and relate to one another. Arlington was an active, dynamic participant in these transformations rather than only a backdrop. All aspects of the county's life, including its governance, social structure, and educational system, were impacted by the technological revolution. It presented Arlington as a microcosm of broader trends, a location where the future frequently appeared a little early and provided insight into the successes and difficulties of living in the digital era.

Chapter 18: Changing Demographics and Culture of the 20th Century to the Millennium

Arlington experienced significant changes as the 20th century came to an end and the new millennium arrived, both culturally and demographically, reflecting broader changes in American society. Arlington saw waves of change that were not isolated rippling effects, but rather pieces of a greater cultural and demographic mosaic that was changing all around the country. As new populations settled in Arlington, they brought a variety of viewpoints, customs, and life experiences that shaped the county's social structure and added to its cultural fabric.

Arlington was mostly a white suburban town in the early 20th century. Significant changes were brought about during the First and Second World Wars. The growth of the Pentagon and the flood of federal employment brought workers from around the nation to Arlington. Although these were mostly white Americans at first, the diversity increased in the ensuing decades.

The 1960s Civil Rights Movement sparked profound societal shifts that eventually permeated every Arlington community, including Arlington's. Abolition of segregation and the enactment of civil rights legislation provided African Americans in the region with new prospects. By the end of the century, Arlington's population was more diversified in terms of race than it had ever been, despite the fact that progress was slow and fraught with difficulties.

Another type of demographic shift occurred during the 1970s and 1980s: immigration. In search of economic possibilities and fleeing political unrest and civil unrest, waves of immigrants from Asia, Africa, and Latin America started to arrive. New languages, customs, and tastes were introduced to the region by Vietnamese, Salvadorans, Ethiopians, and several other groups. Every group made a unique contribution to the town, whether it was through the establishment of companies serving a multicultural clientele or the introduction of new culinary traditions. The influx of immigrants changed Arlington's demographics from mostly monocultural to multicultural and energetic.

The technological boom that followed the turn of the 20th century into the 21st greatly broadened the range of individuals drawn to Arlington. Arlington was becoming a desirable area to live for highly qualified workers from around the globe due to the growing tech industry and the presence of government institutions. Younger, more multicultural crowds were also drawn to the area's universities and colleges.

However, these demographic shifts had cultural ramifications that affected every facet of Arlington society, going beyond simple statistics. This greater diversity was mirrored in the emergence of community organizations, museums, and cultural institutions, as well as in festivals honoring other cultures. Multicultural curricula were introduced into schools, and local companies began to serve a wider range of clientele.

Tensions arose from the change since not everyone was willing or able to adjust to the county's new look. Sometimes concerns about cultural misinterpretations, cheap housing, and educational disparities came up. But they also sparked fruitful dialogues, town hall meetings, and policy deliberations on how to establish an environment that welcomes all Arlingtonians.

By the year 2000, Arlington had developed into a microcosm of the larger changes taking place in the United States. Its streets were a voyage around the globe, with every step exposing a new facet of its incredibly rich and varied culture. Arlington's changing demographic profile was a reflection of the city's changing character; it had become a symbol of the complex, diverse American society of the new millennium. Thus, the history of Arlington provides an invaluable prism through which to view how America is evolving, overcoming new obstacles, and enhancing its cultural legacy.

Chapter 19: Post-9/11 Arlington

Few could have foreseen the events that would drastically change the course of American history and have a significant impact on communities all around the country as the twenty-first century came to an end. On September 11, 2001, Arlington, Virginia experienced an instant and profound shift in its way. The Pentagon incident, which occurred inside Arlington's boundaries, was more than just an attack on the country's military headquarters; it was also a tragedy that happened in the backyards of Arlington citizens, a communal trauma that permeated every residence, community center, and school.

Arlington saw a transformation as a result of the 9/11 communal experience. The attacks increased the emphasis on national security for a county that was already actively involved in military and governmental matters, both locally and in the greater Washington, D.C. metro region. The emotional reconstruction of the town took much longer and had far-reaching effects on its identity and position in both national and international affairs. The Pentagon was reconstructed in an astoundingly short amount of time.

Following 9/11, there was an upsurge in communal cohesiveness. People from all walks of life jumped into action, organizing blood drives, fundraisers, and volunteer opportunities in a flash and providing whatever assistance they could. Despite being overburdened, the local emergency services and medical facilities operated with remarkable efficiency. Memorial ceremonies and candlelight vigils provided venues for group sorrow, illustrating the resiliency and cohesion of a broken but resilient community.

The longer-term modifications held comparable importance. The level of security in public areas, such as schools, retail malls, and transit hubs, has significantly grown. The area's defense and intelligence sectors grew quickly, which brought in a large number of individuals with specialized knowledge in these areas. The actual terrain started to shift: strong gates and concrete obstacles proliferated, serving as a continual reminder of the need for caution.

The public schools in Arlington underwent adjustments as well. More in-depth conversations about politics, history, and ethics—especially in relation to questions of war, peace, and civic duty—began to be incorporated into the curriculum. The goal of developing well-rounded citizens in an increasingly complex society led to a larger emphasis on community service and social studies in after-school programs and extracurricular activities.

Nevertheless, 9/11 exposed long-standing divisions within the community, even as it brought it together in many other ways. The varied population of Arlington was particularly affected by the significant change in federal immigration laws and the expansion of domestic surveillance. Discussions concerning immigrant communities' rights and civil liberties grew increasingly pressing, on family dinner tables as well as local political debates. A complicated and occasionally unsettling social dynamic resulted from the convergence of concerns about personal freedom and communal cohesion with national security considerations.

An especially significant change was how 9/11 affected the functions of Arlington's military installations and bases. Arlington, which was already a major hub for the defense industry, witnessed the growth of military-related infrastructure as well as the influx of more and more military families. The demography of local businesses, schools, and housing markets were all impacted by this. In the meantime, veterans of the subsequent wars in Afghanistan and Iraq started to participate more and more in community life, offering fresh viewpoints to debates concerning Arlington's future course.

Essentially, Arlington's post-9/11 makeover turned it into a microcosm of the country's larger difficulties and changes in the early 21st century. Through tragedy, the community found new sources of resiliency, cohesion, and flexibility, but it also encountered complex new issues associated with its changing identity. Arlington's story in the wake of 9/11 is one of continuity and change at the same time, a complex story that captures the intricacies, conflicts, and hopes of a country trying to find its position in a world that is changing quickly.

Chapter 20: Contemporary Challenges and Opportunities

The history of Arlington, Virginia, provides us with a window into the larger social, economic, and cultural opportunities and problems that face the United States of America in the twenty-first century. This community's canvas is intricately patterned with light and shadow, demonstrating how historical currents continue to influence our experience in the present.

The shortage of affordable housing is one of Arlington's biggest problems. Housing expenses have risen dramatically as the region's computer industry flourishes and more federal contracts come into the area. Undoubtedly, this economic prosperity benefits a large number of people, but it also makes income disparity worse. A neighborhood that some inhabitants have called home for years is becoming more and more expensive for them to live in, especially those who work in services or have fixed incomes. Important conversations about community land trusts, rent controls, and zoning laws—all of which attempt to strike a balance between social equality and growth—have been sparked by this.

The housing market's aftereffects can be seen in Arlington's school system, which is a cause for continuous worry as well as great pride. Even though the county's public schools are frequently praised for providing excellent instruction, there is still a performance disparity that is partially compounded by differences in income. Although early childhood education and improved after-school programs have been instituted as potential remedies, educators, parents, and legislators continue to vigorously discuss them.

Like the rest of the world, Arlington faces significant challenges due to climate change. Prioritizing both short-term solutions and long-term planning is necessary in response to rising temperatures, severe weather, and worries about the water quality of the Potomac River. This has prompted innovative initiatives in public transit and sustainable urban development. Although Arlington is regarded as a leader in these fields, the community is still getting used to the tightrope act of juggling sustainability objectives with the demands of an expanding population.

In Arlington's modern story, technological innovation—always a double-edged sword—also plays a significant role. On the one hand, Arlington is now home to a thriving job market and is recognized as a center for technical innovation because to the influx of tech companies and startups. However, worries about the privacy of personal information, the moral implications of AI, and the possibility of job displacement from automation are becoming more and more common. Town halls, forums, and educational initiatives centered around these topics are now typical, indicating that the community is actively involved in determining its own destiny in the digital age.

Furthermore, Arlington has become receptive to the social justice movement, which has been sparked by national campaigns against systemic racism, gender inequality, and other types of injustice. The county's varied demographic composition adds depth to these conversations by offering a spectrum of viewpoints from past grievances to future inclusive ambitions. Arlington's social fabric has long included community activity, but it has gained fresh life and emphasis lately, with young people frequently leading the way.

Regarding prospects, Arlington's advantageous position and highly educated workforce render it a desirable site for foreign investment and cross-cultural exchanges. The community is richer as a result of these international ties, which may also serve as a model for international collaboration on problems like public health, education, and climate change.

The modern tale of Arlington is fundamentally a human one, composed of nuanced people amidst a constantly shifting environment. The history, current issues, and potential futures all weave together to create a dynamic tapestry that is always being created. It's a tapestry that includes not only the big, obvious strands of historical events and well-known personalities, but also the smaller, more inconspicuous strands of regular people going about their daily lives. This book extends an invitation for you to become involved in this continuous story, to actively contribute in shaping the history of modern Arlington by embracing the chances and overcoming the obstacles.

Chapter 21: Famous Personalities from Arlington

As our investigation of Arlington, Virginia draws to a close, it is important to highlight the people who have come out of this city and have had a lasting impact not only on Arlington but also on the country and the globe at large. Their experiences testify to the powerful confluence of educational quality, cultural influences, and possibilities that Arlington has long been known for.

Let's start with Arlington-born actress Sandra Bullock, who has won multiple Academy Awards. Her ascent to fame in Hollywood represents the caliber of talent that may come from this region, no doubt influenced by the vast social and cultural diversity that characterizes the neighborhood. Along with being a well-known entertainer, Bullock serves as an inspiration for the next generation of Arlington artists due to her notable accomplishments in both movies and philanthropy.

Then there's Arlington-born Katie Couric, another well-known media figure who rose to prominence by being the country's first female solo anchor of a major evening news program. Her journalism career serves as a tribute to the open-mindedness and spirit of inquiry that Arlington's educational institutions strive to inculcate in their pupils. Couric has demonstrated the kind of influence a person from a comparatively tiny town like Arlington can have on the international scene through local reporting to multinational media.

In the fields of science and technology, we have astrophysicist and Nobel Prize winner Dr. John Mather, who attended Arlington public schools. Dr. Mather was one of the principal investigators behind the Cosmic Background Explorer (COBE) satellite, which contributed to the universe's Big Bang theory's confirmation. Here, science instruction at the community schools, along with an atmosphere that encouraged intellectual curiosity, helped develop a mentality that would later help us comprehend the cosmos on a deeper level.

But Arlingtonians have succeeded in more than simply science, journalism, and entertainment. The area has produced notables in politics and public service, such as former US Congressman Tom Davis, who has played a significant role in influencing government and policy. In a similar vein, General Peter Pace, the Chairman of the Joint Chiefs of Staff, was born in Brooklyn and lived in Arlington for large portions of his career. His contribution to military strategy and planning had a significant impact on the country as a whole as well as Arlington, the location of the Pentagon.

What about literature and the arts? The literary community in Arlington has produced writers such as Orson Scott Card, who is most recognized for the science fiction masterpiece "Ender's Game." Card's origins in Arlington attest to the stimulating environment that encourages innovation and creativity across a wide range of fields. His art, which addresses difficult issues of identity, morality, and society, speaks to the complex lives and issues that the people of Arlington truly care about.

Furthermore, these names are only the very beginning. Arlington's neighborhoods have produced countless other professionals, artists, activists, and public officials who were educated there, motivated by the city's strong sense of community, and inspired by the rich cultural diversity. Academics, local legislators, community activists, business executives, and even Olympic athletes are among them; everyone makes a distinct contribution to the fabric of American culture.

It's critical to understand that these people are not anomalies, but rather the products of a society that values education, embraces variety, and promotes a sense of collective responsibility as we examine them.

Their tales contribute to the complex picture of Arlington, a place where every home, community center, and classroom has the capacity to be extraordinary. These well-known individuals, in fact, are both products of Arlington's distinctive setting and active participants in its continuing history, enriching the very soil from which they rose and encouraging a new generation to aim high.

Chapter 22: Arlington as Seen on TV

It's interesting to think about how Arlington has been portrayed in popular media as we examine the city's place in the national consciousness, whether it be through news, television series, or even national courtroom dramas. Some of these depictions are factual and based in reality, while others err on the side of sensationalism or even fiction, but they all serve as a prism through which the general public can view what Arlington stands for.

The portrayal of Arlington on television is one way that it has entered popular culture. Arlington is an ideal backdrop for narratives, whether they are political thrillers or criminal dramas, because of its closeness to the nation's capital. Characters in these series frequently travel through Washington, D.C.'s corridors of power before going back to their homes or other Arlington secondary places. Whether it's a television show like "The West Wing" or spy thrillers that make use of the Pentagon and other federal agencies, Arlington takes on the role of a sort of "supporting actor," adding realism and an actual setting to tales of political intrigue, national security, and governance.

Arlington hasn't always remained mute in these stories, either; on occasion, it has served as the backdrop for real-life dramas that receive widespread media coverage. The defamation trial between Johnny Depp and Amber Heard served as a dramatic illustration of this. Viewers across and beyond were enthralled with this high-profile legal case, which featured allegations of domestic abuse and character assassination between actor Johnny Depp and actress Amber Heard, his ex-wife. The trial was held at the Circuit Court of Arlington, despite the fact that both parties are well-known figures in Hollywood. By selecting this location, which is far from the glitzy lights of Los

Angeles, the proceedings gave a case that was already emotional and under public scrutiny a level of gravity and seriousness.

Why was Arlington selected as the site of this important trial? Though one can only surmise, its standing as an impartial and rigorous court may have played a role. Furthermore, Virginia has strict defamation rules, which may affect the trial's venue based on reputational and character concerns. Reporters and fans of celebrity news traveled to Arlington because of the trial, and as a result, they experienced the city's public areas, courts, and maybe even local restaurants and businesses. Throughout the trial, Arlington was the center of attention for the entire country; it was not a supporting role in a pre-written drama, but rather the central stage of a true story with ramifications for how society perceives matters like as domestic abuse, celebrity, and the legal system in general.

The Johnny Depp vs. Amber Heard trial is just one instance of how Arlington, whether we're talking about political tales, television and film portrayals, or court dramas, becomes a part of the greater American story. The city, which is sometimes viewed as an adjunct of Washington, D.C., has a distinct identity and function in both the real-life dramas that take place in its courtrooms and hallways and the imagined universes that screenwriters create. Arlington has a way of stealing the show and bringing its distinct flavor to the ongoing American story, whether it's behind the scenes of made-up stories or the scene of actual events that capture the public's interest.

Chapter 23: Arlington as Depicted in Literature

Despite being close to the bustle of Washington, D.C., Arlington, Virginia, manages to retain its own distinct identity, one that has frequently been portrayed and reinterpreted in literary works. While movies and television provide broad overviews of a place and period, literature offers a closer look at the subtle details. In the case of Arlington, literature frequently sheds light on the city's many facets, including its history, people, and culture.

Arlington frequently plays two roles in literature: it serves as a setting and a metaphorical area. Because of its proximity to the center of American government, it is an ideal setting for narratives that explore the intricacies of politics and power. Numerous political novels and spy thrillers have used the Pentagon alone as a backdrop or point of reference. But Arlington is more than just its government buildings and establishments; its green spaces and neighborhood hangouts may serve as backdrops for tales of common heroes, love triangles, or complex family relationships.

Historical fiction finds rich ground in the historical landscape of the city. Consider reading books about characters who are caught between the desire for independence and their allegiance to the Crown during the American Revolution. Or go back to the era of the Civil War, when Arlington was undergoing enormous transformations, including the conversion of the Lee estate into a cemetery for Union troops. These pivotal times have been used by authors to craft gripping stories that pit characters against questions of identity, loyalty, and morality against the backdrop of an Arlington that is changing quickly.

However, Arlington's influence on literature extends beyond tales that are set in its immediate vicinity. It is also mentioned as a location that the characters either originate from or want to go to, a place that molds their dreams, anxieties, and aspirations. In one tale, the city might represent middle-class respectability; in another, it might represent the faceless apparatus of government. It might, however, provide a safe refuge for familial and communal love in other tales.

There are times when literary characters are inspired by prominent personalities in Arlington. Heroes from the community, politicians, and prominent citizens may have their lives fabricated, with the essence of their public personas preserved but layers of made-up events, desires, or inner conflicts are added. They merge fiction and reality to create a universe that entices readers with a sense of familiarity and novelty.

Arlington is a microcosm of the United States, representing its tensions and complexities in the setting of American literature. Here, the political and the personal converge, the past has a lasting influence on the present, and the local and the national are inextricably linked. Arlington is more than just a place when viewed through the literary prism; it is an entity with a continuous story arc that is being written by the passage of time. Arlington enters the world of stories, whether via the keyboard of an aspiring author or the pen of an experienced novelist, always enhancing its complex representation in the vast fabric of American literature.

Chapter 24: Iconic Arlington Landmarks and History

Perhaps the Statue of Liberty or the Golden Gate Bridge come to mind when one thinks about famous American landmarks. On the other hand, Arlington, Virginia, has an equally outstanding array of noteworthy locations that act as geographical markers on the American historical chronology. These sites not only influence Arlington's physical landscape but also bear the weight of historical narratives spanning from the country's founding to the present day. Every structure, monument, and historically significant location serves as a kind of public memory, serving as a reminder of the victories, setbacks, and ordinary lives that have had a long-lasting influence on the city and, consequently, the nation.

One of the most famous is Arlington National Cemetery, which was formerly General Robert E. Lee's residence in the Confederacy. Thousands of men and women who served in the American military, including presidents, justices of the Supreme Court, and unidentified soldiers, have found their eternal resting place at this cemetery. With its eternal flame signifying the nation's never-ending appreciation and remembering, the Tomb of the Unknown Soldier at the cemetery is a moving homage to those who have passed away without a name. The process of transforming a former estate owned by the Confederacy into a hallowed area for Union soldiers is symbolic of a country grappling with its polarized past and striving for unity via shared memories.

And lastly, the Pentagon, which serves as the core of American military might. Since its erection during World War II, this five-sided fortress—which now houses the US Department of Defense headquarters—has had a significant impact on world affairs. The Pentagon became permanently entwined with the sad events of

September 11, 2001, when a hijacked jet pierced one of its outer walls. This incident not only made the Pentagon a symbol of American power but also of fragility and resiliency.

Another must-see monument in Arlington is the Marine Corps War Memorial, also referred to as the Iwo Jima Memorial. The sculpture, which shows the raising of the American flag during the Second World War's Battle of Iwo Jima, is a powerful reminder of the bravery and selflessness of the US Marine Corps. It's a place where you can stand and feel the weight of a historical moment immortalized in bronze. You can almost hear the war cries and sense the relief and triumph that the collective group felt from that one act of raising the flag.

Arlington is known for its cultural offerings, including the Signature Theatre, which has won praise on both a regional and national level for its contributions to American theater. Entering the theater immerses you in a dynamic narrative that challenges, amuses, and sparks thought—a living history of artistic expression. It's more than just a venue for performances; it's a landmark where national dialogues about identity, morality, and society meet local artistic expression.

Not to be overlooked are the historical landmarks in the area that are housed in physical buildings. Consider the Arlington Historical Museum, which is located in the former 1891 Hume School. For those who want to know more about the city's complicated past, from its Native American origins to its current position as a thriving, diverse town, this is an essential resource.

As we learn more about the histories of these famous sites, it becomes evident that Arlington plays a significant role in these histories rather than only serving as their backdrop. These sites reflect important turning moments in Arlington's past, each adding a distinct thread to the complex fabric that shapes the city as it is now. They serve as public narratives that each guest or local is welcome to interact with, inquire about, and find moving. The intangible—the real, breathing history of Arlington, Virginia—can be experienced at these places, whether it's through the solemnity of a military memorial or the thunderous cheers of a theater.

Chapter 25: Architecture of Arlington

You might not see the subtle architectural dance that has been choreographed over the years when you stroll through Arlington, Virginia. But if you stop to look, you'll see that the architecture of the city is a kind of visual journal that documents not just the several stages of its growth but also the social and commercial forces that have shaped the terrain. Arlington's architecture is a complex patchwork that relates an interesting tale about the city's evolution through time. From colonial ruins and Civil War-era buildings to art deco influences and soaring modern towers, it all comes together to form this fascinating cityscape.

It is impossible to talk about Arlington's architecture without bringing up its Colonial heritage. The oldest structure in Arlington is the Ball-Sellers House, which dates back to about 1750. This modest wooden building, with its timber frame and steeply pitched roof, is a live example of the opportunities and difficulties that the first inhabitants encountered. Although its architecture is very different from the imposing structures that would follow, it offers a crucial contrast that deepens our comprehension of Arlington's architectural story.

The variety and elegance of the city's buildings increased along with its expansion throughout the 19th century. During the Civil War, many houses embraced the Italianate style, which is characterized by wide eaves, tall, narrow windows, and ornate brackets beneath the roof. Some residential buildings also bear the imprint of Victorian design, with their elaborate timber trim and multi-pronged rooflines. These houses are remnants of a time when aesthetic detail and craftsmanship were highly prized; they stand in stark contrast to some of the more functional buildings that would follow.

Let's go back in time to the early 20th century, when Art Deco and Beaux-Arts influences start to show. These architectural styles are most likely best shown in a few of Arlington's theaters and government structures. These opulent, richly ornamented buildings capture the optimism and prosperity of post-World War II America, when the country sought to project an image of modernity, progress, and culture.

But as the 20th century progressed, Arlington's architectural environment saw a radical transformation. The emergence of the automobile and the growth of federal offices in Northern Virginia led to the development of what are now known as the residential and commercial high-rises that are the main feature of communities like Rosslyn and Crystal City. During this time, concrete and glass were frequently used as the main building materials, and clean, utilitarian designs were favored in modernist architecture. The simple, angular façades reflect a culture that values functionality and economy over ostentatious beauty.

And then there are the anomalies, the attempts at architecture that are difficult to classify. Consider the 127-foot-tall steel tower known as the Netherlands Carillon, which the Dutch gave to the United States as a thank you for their assistance during and after World War II. Its interesting fusion of modernist and traditional iconography depicts a post-war world in which the past and future were engaged in a dynamic interplay.

However, Arlington's architectural history is far from over. As we enter the twenty-first century, LEED-certified structures that put an emphasis on environmental responsibility demonstrate a resurgence of interest in sustainable construction. Additionally, mixed-use developments are making a comeback. These projects aim to harmoniously combine public, business, and residential areas; they may be a nod to the early Arlington communities' reliance on one another.

Thus, Arlington's architecture is more than just a collection of buildings used for habitation, employment, or tourism. Engraved in brick, wood, glass, and steel is an intricate story. This is a story about needs, priorities, and tastes that change throughout time. Every structure, be it a contemporary skyscraper or a centuries-old house, is a chapter in a continuous tale that we are encouraged to read carefully and, in doing so, to better comprehend Arlington as a whole.

Chapter 26: Key Industries of Economic Evolution

These days, when we talk about Arlington, Virginia, pictures of modern high-rises and busy cityscapes may come to mind. With government contracts and federal agencies dotting the landscape, the federal government looms large, both literally and figuratively. But in order to get here, Arlington had to go through a number of economic changes, each characterized by particular sectors that shaped the city's social and cultural character in addition to its financial profile.

Like most of America, Arlington's economy was mostly based on agriculture in the early years. Tiny farms dot the terrain, yielding a variety of products, such as corn and tobacco. Farming was a way of life that shaped the early settlers' lives and the original character of the area, not just a means of subsistence. Arlington's older neighborhoods, with their historic homes, nevertheless pay homage to its rural heritage.

Arlington saw the rise of mills and small manufacturing businesses in the 19th century as the country progressed toward industrialization. Being close to the Potomac River allowed for the efficient use of water power, while the development of railroads in the surrounding areas allowed for the efficient movement of commodities. Although Arlington never achieved the same level of industrial center status as places like Pittsburgh or Detroit, these early industrial endeavors laid the groundwork for the city's eventual urbanization.

There were major changes brought about by the Civil War. The war not only caused economic devastation in the South but also sparked a change in focus toward new industries. The Civil War era saw the construction of military forts and installations, which signaled the start of a trend that would significantly alter Arlington's economic environment: the blending of the city's and the federal government's fortunes.

During World Wars I and II, when the need for government services and the defense sector skyrocketed, this partnership reached unprecedented heights. One of the most recognizable government structures in Arlington, the Pentagon, came to represent this change in the economy. Built as a logistical marvel during the early stages of World War II, it cemented Arlington's position as a center for military organization and planning. Contracts from the government and military began rolling in, which fueled an increase in employment and population.

As the 20th century went on, Arlington's economy started to diversify. The Information Age introduced technology companies and consulting services into the mix, even though the federal government and military continued to be the dominant employment. The city became a center for specialist services, including engineering knowledge and legal counsel. Businesses needing specialist knowledge found it to be an appealing site due to its emphasis on education and highly qualified workforce.

We've witnessed a shift in recent years toward even greater economic diversification. Arlington's close proximity to Washington, D.C. and abundance of historical landmarks have contributed to the region's tremendous growth in the service, hotel, and tourism industries. The local economy also benefits greatly from the retail and healthcare sectors.

Companies that use green technologies and renewable energy have begun to settle in Arlington as a nod to environmental sustainability and the future. In addition to attracting these kinds of businesses, the city's dedication to sustainability also paves the way for emerging economic trends.

From its agrarian beginnings to its industrial rise, from wartime requirements to peacetime diversification, and from a local focus to being a part of the globalized world, Arlington's economic trajectory is, in many respects, a microcosm of larger American tendencies. However, every phase of this development has left its imprint on Arlington, affecting its architecture, defining its personality, and adding to its intricate and multidimensional identity. The city now serves as a symbol of the various ways that industries both influence and are influenced by the areas in which they are located.

Chapter 27: Arlington in the National and Global Economy

Arlington presents a captivating story of adaptability, interconnectedness, and resilience when viewed in the larger context of both national and global economics. Arlington is more than simply a city in Virginia; it is an essential hub in an expansive global network of politics, trade, innovation, and culture that reaches not only the US but the entire globe.

Arlington's symbiotic relationship with the federal government is crucial to understanding Arlington's role in the national economy. Serving as the home of numerous government departments and contractors, including the Pentagon and the Department of Defense's headquarters, Arlington is a major hub for homeland security, policymaking, and military preparation. Because of its closeness to Washington, D.C., the city is a prime destination for think tanks and other organizations with ties to the government, which have a big influence on national and even international policy.

However, Arlington's contribution to the US economy goes beyond its association with the federal government. It is competitive in industries ranging from information technology to healthcare because to its highly educated workforce and position as a hub for technology and consultancy organizations. Arlington is a hub for innovation and discussion because businesses and organizations there participate in national discussions on issues ranging from environmental sustainability to cybersecurity.

However, the city plays a vital role not just in the national economy but also in the global economy. Because of its workforce's notable diversity, it draws talent from all over the world. This global flavor serves as a competitive advantage rather than merely being a demographic feature.

Arlington-based businesses benefit from a diverse range of cultural viewpoints and skill sets that provide them a competitive advantage in the global marketplace.

Globalization is a reciprocal process. International businesses have made significant investments in Arlington, particularly in the fields of information technology, defense, and policy consulting. Consequently, the city turns into a hub where local and global influences converge, fostering a vibrant and diverse atmosphere that supports both cultural and economic development.

Another important factor in integrating Arlington into the world economy is trade. It is a logistics hub due to its advantageous placement along important road and aviation lines. The flow of people and goods is facilitated by the connections that Washington Dulles International Airport and Ronald Reagan Washington National Airport provide to locations all over the world.

Arlington's prominence in policy circles also gives it a role in solving issues with an international reach, as problems like socioeconomic inequality, climate change, and geopolitical instability take on a more global dimension. With their participation in international alliances, holding of symposiums, and writings for global policy papers, the city's institutions have a significant impact on international affairs.

The most intriguing aspect of Arlington's place in the US and international economies may be its capacity for change and adaptation. Over the course of its history, the main industries in this city have changed multiple times: from agricultural to manufacturing to government to technology and services now. Every change has necessitated adaptation, not just in terms of the type of work that people perform but also in terms of their collaborative and thought processes as well as how they see the place of their community within broader economic frameworks.

Arlington is a microcosm of the larger economic tendencies of the twenty-first century, which include the shift to a knowledge-based economy, the growing interconnectedness of local and global challenges, and the necessity of adaptation in the face of rapid change. It serves as evidence that small communities do not have to be helpless objects of the will of other forces, but can actively participate in national and international economic systems. As a result, researching Arlington's changing place in these bigger economies offers perspective on the city as a whole as well as a way to comprehend the intricately interwoven global economy of today.

Chapter 28: Notable Companies in Arlington

Examining Arlington's business scene requires highlighting the illustrious corporations that have established themselves in this thriving Virginia city, just a short distance from the capital of the United States. These businesses range from those with a strong foundation in government and defense contracts to those at the forefront of innovation, technology, and social impact. When taken as a whole, they represent Arlington's many diverse qualities and act as cornerstones of its economic health.

Let us begin by addressing the topic that is often overlooked: government contracts. Owing to its close proximity to Washington, D.C., Arlington serves as a central hub for federal government-related firms. Lockheed Martin is unique among them all. The U.S. Department of Defense counts this aerospace and defense corporation among its major contractors. It is synonymous with programs including anything from missile defense systems to cutting-edge combat jets. The location of Lockheed Martin in Arlington denotes the city's significance in the intersection of politics, defense, and technology.

Another significant company in the defense industry is General Dynamics. The company is an example of how many government-contracting firms in Arlington have grown diversified. It provides a wide range of products and services in the areas of information technology, combat systems, and aerospace. Its impact extends beyond the military into fields like cybersecurity and communications infrastructure, demonstrating the breadth of work done by these Arlington, Virginia-based firms.

Arlington, though, is more than just a federal contractors' playground. Technology and consultancy organizations also have a strong presence there. This location is home to offices of firms such as Accenture and Deloitte, which provide a broad range of consulting services to clients in the public and private sectors. Their existence attests to Arlington's capacity to draw in highly educated and competent laborers, who are essential for the strategic thinking and problem-solving these consultancies provide.

Arlington is also home to a thriving tech community. Amazon selected Arlington as one of the locations for its second headquarters, or HQ2, in a highly publicized decision. The decision by the e-commerce behemoth was a huge victory for the city, as it would bring with it a plethora of jobs and future economic growth. However, the presence of Amazon also reflects something more profound: it confirms the city's increasing standing as an innovative and talented East Coast technology hub.

Arlington is home to smaller, highly influential businesses in addition to these enormous corporations, particularly in the fields of social entrepreneurship, healthcare, and renewable energy. Businesses that support a greener, more sustainable future include Opower, which specializes in customer engagement platforms for utility providers with the goal of encouraging energy-saving behavior. These smaller firms frequently form alliances with larger ones, fostering the development of a regional ecosystem that fosters innovation.

Acknowledging these companies' significance in forming Arlington's local and regional character is crucial. These are not just companies operating alone; rather, they represent pieces of a greater social fabric. They increase the tax base, create jobs, have an impact on local laws, and frequently participate in charitable endeavors that directly help the Arlington community.

Furthermore, these businesses work hand in hand with the city's other resources, which include its highly educated populace, well-developed transportation system, and universities and research facilities. When combined, they create a dynamic, multi-layered economic environment in which each component strengthens the others.

Knowing Arlington means knowing its businesses, which range from agile tech startups to dependable defense contractors. These businesses serve as both a window into Arlington's past and a predictor of its future, demonstrating the city's ongoing adaptation and its significance on the local, state, and even international arenas. So, when we look at these noteworthy businesses, we see more than just a roster of corporate names—rather, we see a story of a city that is always moving, purposefully moving.

Chapter 29: Visual Art and Movements in Arlington

Visual art plays a colorful and dynamic role in Arlington's rich history and culture, one that is sometimes ignored yet greatly adds to the city's distinct personality. In fact, Arlington is more than just a background of government buildings and cutting-edge businesses—it's a living, breathing canvas on which numerous artistic movements have left their lasting imprints.

As varied as the city itself, Arlington's visual arts sector features a wide range of artistic materials, styles, and meanings. This city has featured a variety of art genres over the years, including installation art, painting, sculpture, murals, and digital media, all of which speak to the diverse population and represent larger trends in American art history. Communities come together to create, appreciate, and discuss art in a number of the city's public spaces, galleries, and art centers, which act as hubs for both artists and art enthusiasts.

A mainstay of this cultural environment is the Arlington Arts Center, which is housed in a historic structure that was constructed in the late 19th century. This organization provides a venue for established and up-and-coming artists to exhibit their work as well as an instructional center. The Arts Center captures the spirit of the times with its carefully chosen exhibitions that frequently address current topics ranging from social justice to environmental concerns, establishing art as a vital component of public conversation in Arlington.

Arlington's visual art trends also heavily incorporate public art, which has an equally powerful influence. A means of expressing common culture, public art takes many forms, from murals illuminating urban areas to sculptures gracing public squares. Initiatives like the Crystal City Underground Mural Project involve local artists in converting normally functional rooms into works of art that embody the spirit of the city. Beyond merely improving the environment, these initiatives democratize art by making it available to all locals, regardless of their background or level of artistic training.

Design on the ART Another notable program is Buses. This program, as its name implies, turns regular public buses into moving art exhibits, presenting local artists' creations to commuters. Here, the lines separating public area from art gallery serve as a reminder that art in Arlington is a shared, community experience.

In the field of digital arts, Arlington has also adapted and changed quickly. Arlington-based artists have been eager to experiment with the new artistic mediums that the development of technology has brought forth. Arlington's receptive and passionate audience for technology-based artistic practices, which range from digital painting and graphic design to video art, is indicative of the city's progressive and inventive nature.

Remarkably, the city's art sector has also been inclusive, making sure that the experiences and narratives of its varied populace are shown. African American, Asian, and Latino artists have become more well-known, tackling subjects like cultural heritage and the experience of immigration. Their creations give Arlington's artistic environment unique textures that complement the diversity of the community they serve.

The colleges and universities in the Arlington area are crucial in fostering the next wave of artists. They instill a love of art in young people through comprehensive arts education programs and partnerships with neighborhood art institutions, guaranteeing that the city's creative culture is vibrant and ever-evolving.

Arlington's visual arts are an essential means of expression and communication that add to the city's nuanced personality; they are not an afterthought. Art in Arlington is thought-provoking, stimulating, and enlightening whether it is seen in a gallery or on a bus. It is a window and a mirror, reflecting the many faces of the community and providing a doorway to new perspectives. It provides a place where individuals can gather and partake in the fundamental human activity of interpreting shape and color. By doing this, it enriches Arlington, Virginia's complex and fascinating story with yet another dimension.

Chapter 30: Music and Musical Movements in Arlington

When it comes to Arlington's musical landscape, you're entering an area where harmonies are created by fusing history, culture, and a feeling of place. This chapter pays tribute to Arlington, Virginia's richly varied and complex musical landscape. Arlington has forged its own distinct musical identity, mirroring the various musical traditions of the country while adding its own notes to the American symphony, and it is far more than just Washington, D.C.'s neighbor.

Arlington's music is a mixture, an assemblage of various sounds, cultures, and historical periods, much like the rest of the country. The essence of blues, jazz, classical, rock, punk, country, hip-hop, and electronic music has been caught in local venues, resonated via community gatherings, and performed by both amateur and professional performers. These genres have all had their moments in the spotlight.

Live music was a common component of community fairs, church gatherings, and local events in Arlington's early years, serving as a source of entertainment and camaraderie. This is where the city's musical history began. The region's need for a wider variety of musical styles increased as it expanded. Early 20th-century jazz did not ignore Arlington; in fact, the neighborhood boasted its own jazz clubs, providing a suburban counterbalance to the thriving D.C. jazz scene. The blues also made a comfortable home in Arlington, frequently in settings that promoted impromptu jam sessions where performers would craft complex tunes long into the night.

Arlington was hardly an exception during the mid-20th century rock 'n' roll fever that swept the country. Rock bands thrived in the local theaters and teen clubs, and some of them went on to become well-known throughout the region or perhaps the country. Not to be outdone, the punk scenes of the 1970s and 1980s also made a lasting impression, converting some Arlington venues into sacred spaces for musical revolt.

As we move closer to the present, electronic dance music (EDM) and hip-hop have also taken turns ruling the stage. Arlington was frequently engulfed in the musical currents reshaping the nation's capital due to its close proximity to Washington, D.C. Originating in D.C., go-go music is a style of funk that resonated across the Potomac and found eager listeners in Arlington's nightclubs and community festivals.

This musical scene is further enhanced by Arlington's rich cultural tapestry. While traditional Asian and Middle Eastern music can be heard at cultural events and even in some local restaurants, Latino music genres like reggaeton and salsa have been recognized in the city's cultural festivals.

But the locations where this music is performed are just as fascinating as the range of genres that make Arlington's musical scene so alluring. Every musical taste can be satisfied in a setting that ranges from cozy coffee cafes with acoustic shows to larger venues big enough to hold orchestras. While live bands from a variety of genres frequently play in Clarendon's neighborhood bars, musical theater is presented in venues such as the Signature Theatre.

Maintaining Arlington's musical culture also depends heavily on music education. Strong music programs are provided by the local schools, guaranteeing that the upcoming generation of artists will receive the necessary technical training and creative support. In addition, a number of private teachers and music schools provide specialized instruction in everything from electronic music production to classical piano.

Every chapter of Arlington's history, as we have seen throughout this book, is intricate and multi-layered, and its musical story is no different. Arlington's music culture is a dynamic and ever-evolving phenomenon, from a string quartet playing a Beethoven piece in a formal theater to a local indie band playing original songs in a darkly lit pub. It is an essential component of the community's spirit, a vibrant, constantly-evolving soundtrack to a never-still metropolis.

Chapter 31: Other Cultural Festivals in Arlington

Calendars brimming with cultural festivals that explode with vibrancy, color, and the heartfelt rhythms of varied traditions may be found in Arlington. We've looked at Arlington from the perspectives of its politics, economy, history, and even musical landscape, but we also need to consider the city as a hub for cultural events. These festivals are significant representations of the city's cosmopolitan spirit, encapsulating the spirit of its multinational terrain, rather than merely fleeting events that end when the stage is taken down and the food vendors pack up.

Consider the Arlington Festival of the Arts, for instance. Every year, the Clarendon district is transformed into an outdoor art gallery for this festival, which features hundreds of artists from all across the region and beyond. You can discover a colorful assortment of paintings, sculptures, photos, and even interactive works as you stroll around the neighborhood. Purchasing art is not the only thing to do; you need also get to know the viewpoints and creative expressions of individuals whose experiences may be very different from your own.

The Columbia Pike Blues Festival is another option, one that welcomes both blues enthusiasts and beginners. The festival was first created as a way to honor the rich history of American blues music, but it has expanded to feature other genres as well, increasing its audience and reach. Its dedication to community involvement never wavers; neighborhood companies and associations frequently take part, giving the occasion an even more uniquely local feel.

The Turkish Festival is a multi-sensory extravaganza of traditional music, folk dances, and a broad selection of food vendors serving delectable treats like kebabs and baklava. The festival offers more than just food; it's a bridge between cultures, showcasing traditional crafts, Turkish history, and language classes for those who want to learn more about the country.

Arlington's annual Latino American Festival honors the city's Latino community as well. This festival highlights the distinctive cultures of many nations via dance, music, and cuisine. Enjoying a pupusa, witnessing a salsa dancer, or listening to a mariachi band are all examples of interacting with a population that has greatly influenced Arlington's social and cultural landscape.

Without including Arlington's Lunar New Year celebrations, no overview of its cultural festivals would be complete. With an increasing Asian American population, the city welcomes the lunar new year with fireworks, traditional lion dances, and the distribution of auspicious red envelopes, or "hongbao."

Lastly, the Rosslyn Jazz Festival merits recognition for its capacity to unite people around a shared enjoyment of the arts in addition to its musical offerings. This festival, which draws a crowd as eclectic as the music itself, features local and worldwide jazz performers against the backdrop of Arlington's skyscrapers and the Potomac River.

These festivals capture the spirit of a city that lives on diversity and connectivity, serving as miniature versions of Arlington's larger cultural landscape. Every festival is more than a day or two; it's a part of the story of the city, one chapter in an ongoing tale that pays tribute to the past while actively interacting with the present. Each reflects the patchwork of histories and identities that make up Arlington itself, providing not just amusement but also an education in the complexities and beauties of various cultures. Arlington people weave together the strands of mutual respect and shared community to create a tapestry rich in color and exquisite design through laughter, music, dance, and even the shared experience of eating novel food.

Chapter 32: Key Educational Institutions

Arlington is home to numerous educational institutions that are pillars of knowledge and advancement in addition to monuments honoring politics, history, and culture. In addition to offering formal education, these colleges, universities, and other educational institutions make significant and enduring contributions to the city's intellectual, social, and cultural fabric. Owing to Arlington's location near the nation's capital, policy, governance, and global concerns are frequently infused into the curriculum, making it vital.

In Arlington, it is nearly impossible to discuss education without bringing up the public school system. For similar schools in Virginia and around the country, Arlington Public Schools (APS) serves as an example. Notable are the district's emphasis on advanced placement classes, STEM (Science, Technology, Engineering, and Math) curricula, and programs that promote cultural diversity. Yorktown High School and Washington-Liberty High School, for example, have won awards for their comprehensive curricula that educate students for the difficulties of the twenty-first century and for their academic achievement.

However, APS is made up of more than just academically challenging high schools; it also includes establishments such as the Arlington Career Center, which provides both specialized career and technical programs and a demanding academic curriculum. The goal here is to give pupils a well-rounded set of abilities that will prepare them for college and the workforce; this is a comprehensive approach that sets Arlington's educational system apart.

Higher education campuses are also located in Arlington. The Arlington campus of George Mason University is especially noteworthy. Among its many specialized departments are the Antonin

Scalia Law School and the Schar School of Policy and Government, both of which are housed in the Virginia Square neighborhood. Because of its close proximity to Washington, D.C., the university is able to maintain strong relationships with governmental, non-profit, and private sector groups, providing students with an educational experience that few universities can match in terms of real-world exposure.

Additionally present in Arlington are the many campuses of the Northern Virginia Community College (NOVA), which caters to a diverse student body from a range of backgrounds. Many students use it as a stepping stone before transferring to four-year universities because of its strong two-year programs.

Arlington is home to a multitude of specialist training facilities and educational institutions in addition to these conventional classrooms. For example, the international Service Institute provides training for individuals working in international affairs and diplomacy, while the several defense contractors in the region frequently offer internal training programs for their staff members. These specialized training programs serve as an example of Arlington's function within the broader framework of US foreign policy, military, and administration.

Of course, Arlington offers more than just formal education. Public debate forums, free classes, and community education initiatives are offered by libraries such as the Arlington Central Library. Workshops and classes in anything from computer programming to the arts are available at a number of different community centers located throughout the city.

Arlington fosters a culture of lifelong learning through these organizations, where gaining knowledge is viewed as both an individual pursuit and a collective duty of the community. This viewpoint is in perfect harmony with the city's long history of civic engagement, activism, and intellectual integrity—all of which are embedded in the dynamic social and technical environments of modern-day America. Arlington's educational institutions strive to develop knowledgeable citizens who can effectively traverse the intricacies of a global society and make meaningful contributions to their local communities, in addition to producing academically proficient pupils. These institutions serve as centers of intellectual and innovative activity, each one writing a new chapter in the ongoing narrative of a city that cherishes the intellectual lives of its citizens just as much as its varied and rich past.

Chapter 33: Arlington's Role in Academia and Research

The intellectual landscape of Arlington, Virginia, is rich and reaches far beyond the confines of the classroom to include cutting-edge research and scholarly dialogue. Situated between numerous esteemed colleges and the intellectual hubs of Washington, D.C., Arlington holds a distinct position as a center for scholarly endeavors and research. The city now plays a more significant role in academics than just being a participant; it shapes and leads conversations in a wide range of academic fields.

It's easy to think of research initially in terms of the hard sciences, and Arlington has made significant contributions in these areas as well. AI, cybersecurity, and aerospace engineering are just a few of the domains where research is strongly supported due to the large presence of government-funded initiatives and defense contractors. Public-private sector cooperation thrive in this environment. For example, in order to bridge the gap between theoretical investigation and real-world application, academia researchers frequently work with engineers in nearby tech companies.

But Arlington's scholarly contributions have considerably wider applicability. The city enjoys a unique edge in the social sciences, especially in fields like international relations, political science, and policy studies, because of its proximity to the political center of the United States. Organizations like the Schar School of Policy and Government at George Mason University conduct applied research that is immediately relevant to the country's legislative and diplomatic efforts in addition to traditional academic studies. Similarly, the numerous think tanks and research facilities dispersed around the city frequently offer the crucial intellectual foundation for proposed laws and foreign policy choices, adding a level of academic rigor to the frequently chaotic realm of politics.

The field of medical research in Arlington is also noteworthy, especially in light of its ties to the armed forces and veterans. Research endeavors frequently concentrate on fields such as prosthetics, rehabilitative medicine, and PTSD (post-traumatic stress disorder). Wide-ranging effects result from the work done here, helping not only the military community but also civilians.

In addition, the city is home to a wide range of archives, collections, and libraries that are invaluable to academics. These places are more than just book storage facilities; they are centers of learning that foster inquiry and discussion, whether it is a doctoral student poring over old manuscripts at the Arlington Central Library or an experienced scholar using specialized government papers.

Additionally, Arlington provides a forum for scholarly discourse by way of public lectures, symposia, and academic conferences. These conferences bring together intellectuals from all around the world, providing a forum for idea exchange, orthodoxy challenges, and the creation of new intellectual relationships. Organizing academic events in Arlington typically imbues the proceedings with an additional sense of gravity and urgency, owing to its advantageous location and easy access to governmental agencies.

Notably, Arlington's contribution to academics is not limited to its adult population alone. Its youngest citizens benefit from its dedication to academic success. Science fairs, debating tournaments, and history projects are a few ways that local schools are fostering research aptitude and raising awareness of the intellectual capacity and responsibility of the next generation.

Arlington's emphasis on scholarly study contributes to the city's reputation as a hub of knowledgeable, critical thought in a larger cultural sense. The city serves as a reminder of the value of thorough investigation and reasoned discussion in a world where oversimplified narratives and polarizing ideologies are becoming more prevalent. This city's intellectual ecology is an essential component that supports its social, cultural, and civic life rather than just an add-on to its other operations. Arlington leaves a lasting impression on the academic community through its public places, research facilities, schools, and universities. It also advances research that has an impact much beyond Arlington's borders.

Chapter 34: Natural Disasters in Arlington and their Impact

Perhaps the last thing that springs to mind when thinking of Arlington, Virginia, is natural disasters. Arlington rarely finds itself in the direct path of devastating natural events, in contrast to communities that are subject to earthquakes on the Pacific coast or hurricanes along the coastline. The city is not completely shielded from the elements, though. Not only have floods, violent storms, and sporadic earthquakes jolted Arlington's physical infrastructure, but they have also had profound social and political ramifications.

The most frequent of these occurrences has been flooding, which is partially explained by Arlington's urbanization and close proximity to bodies of water like the Potomac River. Flooding events over the years have forced the local administration to reevaluate development regulations and zoning laws. Following significant floods, the focus of discussion frequently turns to stormwater management, sewage system upgrades, and low-lying area protection. For those involved in urban planning and environmental conservation who are considering the relationship between ecological sustainability and urban growth, these occurrences can be used as case studies. Flooding turns from being merely a natural calamity to a starting point for conversations about how to build a city that coexists peacefully with its environment.

Severe storms have also affected Arlington, including tropical storms and hurricane remnants that have periodically moved up the East Coast. Such incidents frequently highlight weak points in the city's infrastructure in the wake of them. For instance, power outages reveal the limitations of an electrical grid that is being put to the test more and more by the needs of a growing population and the unpredictable nature of climate change. They also cause brief inconveniences. When something like this happens, the public conversation usually shifts to updating infrastructure—not simply to get it back to how it was before, but also to get it ready for new challenges.

Even though they are uncommon, earthquakes have occurred throughout Arlington's history along with other natural disasters, such as the 2011 Virginia earthquake that was felt all the way up the East Coast. Even though the incident only caused modest physical harm to the surrounding area, Arlingtonians' mental state was forever altered. The earthquake abruptly expanded the range of scenarios that locals thought likely, which in turn prompted a fresh emphasis on disaster preparedness that extended beyond weather-related events. Residents were taught how to secure their homes and workplaces against seismic shocks, and earthquake exercises were conducted in offices and schools.

Natural disasters also highlight issues of social justice and inequality in a larger societal context. The most vulnerable groups are almost always the ones that suffer the most since they don't have the resources to appropriately prepare for or recover from such occurrences. Following every major incident, advocacy groups and community organizations find a newfound purpose in drawing attention to these inequities and advocating for the equitable distribution of resources for disaster preparation and recovery.

Natural catastrophes have an effect on Arlington that extends beyond the short time after they occur. They set off a series of events that have long-term effects on public policy, civic participation, and social connections. With every calamity, a layer of the city's façade is peeled back to expose strengths and flaws that might not otherwise be noticeable. They issue a challenge to both citizens and legislators to reconsider what it means to be a resilient city in the twenty-first century.

Therefore, even though Arlington isn't exactly the center of catastrophic natural disasters, the events that do occur there do act as triggers for reflection and change. They have left a lasting impression on the city's collective memory and future development since they are woven into its social and political fabric. Arlington's experience with natural disasters is therefore a microcosm of how communities around the country might use hardship as a tool to drive themselves toward a more egalitarian and sustainable future.

Chapter 35: History of Sports and Athletes from Arlington

Sports are more than just recreational activity in Arlington, Virginia; they are an integral part of the community's social fabric and sense of identity. Like in a lot of America, Arlington's sports are more than just contests; they serve as venues for civic involvement, neighborhood pride, and the individual and group quest of excellence. The history of sports in Arlington, from neighborhood Little Leagues to renowned Olympians, tells much about the goals and ideals of the community as well as the complex relationship between regional history and larger American influences.

Arlington has a lengthy history with baseball, spanning from backyard games to more organized Little League leagues. On fields like Barcroft Park, young people from the area have spent many innings honing their craft, developing not just their athletic prowess but also a feeling of community and lifetime friendships. Some of these young people, like sports analyst and former Major League baseball player David Aldridge, have gone on to have successful careers in the major leagues. These athletes' careers provide evidence of strong community support, local mentorship, and a work ethic that emphasizes fair play and diligence.

Like football, basketball has a fervent fan base that enjoys playing it for fun and competitively. With fierce rivalries that crowd gyms and serve as a breeding ground for talent that might one day adorn college or even professional courts, local high schools frequently operate as the crucible for upcoming talents. For young basketball aspirants, the career accomplishments of Arlington native Dennis Scott, who had a significant NBA career, serve as motivation, proving that goals conceived on Arlington courts may, in fact, reach extraordinary heights.

If team sports like basketball and baseball create the foundation for social engagement within the community, then individual sports like gymnastics and swimming have provided Arlington's athletes with a stage on which to excel. Many talented young people train for hours at Arlington's gyms and aquatic centers; some of them go on to compete nationally or even at the Olympics. These particular endeavors, which frequently call for a remarkable level of dedication from athletes and their families, highlight another important but distinct aspect of Arlington's sports culture: a concentration on individual greatness and the virtues of self-control and tenacity.

But the tale of sports in Arlington isn't only about the players; it's also about the supporters and spectators who offer a special fusion of fervor and decorum to the stands. Local sporting events provide as a platform for the community to gather together, for businesses in the area to display their wares, and for all ages to experience a sense of belonging. And it's not just about traditional sports either; Arlington has welcomed a wide variety of sports, from skateboarding to cycling to soccer, each with a devoted fan base.

Arlington's sports scene has changed and evolved over time, mirroring larger cultural shifts. For example, the development of organized women's sports leagues during the last half of the 20th century, prompted by Title IX-related laws, was a major turning point for both gender equality and the enhancement of the regional sports landscape. In a similar vein, as Arlington's population becomes more diverse, more sports are becoming popular. Two such sports are cricket and soccer, which reflect the city's rising South Asian and Hispanic communities.

In this sense, Arlington's sports past serves as a window into greater social, cultural, and even political tendencies. From neighborhood games to professional sports with big stakes, the pursuit of success, fair play, and community development never wavers. Arlington's fields, courts, and swimming pools serve as more than just places to play sports; they are settings for the various stories that the city's residents have to tell, each one weaving into a bigger picture that depicts Arlington's history. So long as a child is playing soccer for the first time or an athlete representing their country at the national level, sports will always be a vital part of Arlington, Virginia's history.

Chapter 36: Noteworthy Recreational Spaces

In a fast-paced, dynamic city like Arlington, Virginia, parks and green areas are priceless havens where locals can take a moment to unwind, breathe, and get back in touch with the local environment and each other. These areas are not merely playgrounds or patches of greenery; rather, they are intricately intertwined into Arlington's history and culture, each with an own narrative that speaks to people of all ages.

Consider the well-known Arlington National Cemetery. Not only is it a military cemetery and a memorial to the men and women who served, but it's also a place where people go to reflect in peace. on addition to offering a lesson on the history of the country, the immaculately kept grounds, dotted with memorials and significant places like the Tomb of the Unknown Soldier, also offer a place for introspection. Here, the distinctions between a historical site, a public space, and a recreational area blend together to represent the diverse identities that shape Arlington's unique character.

Then there's the adored Theodore Roosevelt Island, an 88.5-acre natural reserve honoring the country's 26th president. This park provides a peaceful haven from the bustle of the city with its walking routes winding through woodland areas and a statue honoring Roosevelt's commitment to conservation. The island honors a conservationist President, but it's also a place where people can go running, go bird watching, or just hang out by the water's edge. It's a live example of the community's commitment to environmental principles.

Potomac Overlook Regional Park is another excellent illustration of how Arlington's recreational areas have several uses. The park is a natural haven for flora and fauna, including approximately 70 acres of sanctuary that spans forests, creeks, and meadows. But if you dig a little farther, you'll uncover a wealth of knowledge. With its Organic Vegetable Garden, Ecosystems Exhibit, and even a bird of prey exhibit, the park turns weekend getaways into educational adventures. Hence, the park functions as an outdoor school where culture and environment meet, providing for a varied recreational experience that benefits the body and mind.

Talk about Arlington's parks and trails and it wouldn't be complete without bringing up its vast system of walking and bicycling paths. For instance, the Custis and Mount Vernon Trails, which connect important locations like the George Washington Memorial Parkway and other communities, offer an unmatched perspective to take in the area's natural splendor. These trails embody the ethos of a community that promotes environmental care and active living; they are more than just walkways. They demonstrate a dedication to sustainable urban development that places a high priority on wellness, accessibility, and sustainability—values that are fundamental to Arlington's community spirit.

Arlington's recreational areas double as venues for athletic events, cultural festivals, and community gatherings. These are the locations where the community comes to life, whether it's at the Arlington Mill Community Center's farmers' market, Gateway Park in Rosslyn, or Long Bridge Park for kids' soccer matches. These are the spaces that hold the happy, ordinary, and occasionally life-changing events that collectively shape what it means to live in Arlington.

It is important to remember that these parks have served as activist and social change hotspots. Previously segregated areas like Quincy Park served as civil rights battlegrounds, mirroring the broader national movement for equality. In addition to serving as a reminder of the work that still to be done, the ultimate desegregation of these parks represents the progress that has been made.

In the end, Arlington's green areas are more than just pieces of ground; they are little representations of the ideals, aspirations, and shared history of the neighborhood. They are communal living rooms where friendships are made, a collective canvas on which the colors of the seasons are painted, and a communal haven of comfort and creativity. By distilling the spirit of these areas, one learns more about Arlington's innermost thoughts and feelings than just the landscape. In addition to serving as the city's green lung, these parks, trails, and open spaces also serve as its beating heart, preserving the various historical, cultural, and social tales that contribute to Arlington, Virginia's complexity and never-ending fascination.

Chapter 37: Noteworthy Nature in Arlington

Surrounding Arlington is a breathtaking natural beauty that perfectly complements the rich tapestry of the city's history and culture. Tucked away from the glitz of skyscrapers, memorials, and highways are pockets of unyielding natural beauty that add their own unique tones of green to Arlington's vibrant landscape. Arlington successfully blends the vibrancy of natural life with the built environment, setting it apart from other cities that are drab, asphalt expanses. This makes Arlington an intriguing place for naturalists, outdoor lovers, historians, and urban explorers alike.

The Potomac River tributary known as Four Mile Run is a superb example of Arlington's natural resilience. Even though it was once a dead, dirty stream, restoration efforts have turned it into a living example of environmental management. Here, one may see a variety of fish species swimming through the currents, great blue herons patrolling the shallow waters, and beavers building their elaborate dams. Botany fans can enjoy a variety of native plants, from the strong oak to the ephemeral spring ephemerals like trillium and Virginia bluebells, at the neighboring Four Mile Run Park, which boasts rich vegetation and walking pathways.

Named for the creek that runs through it, Donaldson Run Park is another urban oasis of natural beauty. Those who are interested in studying aquatic ecosystems will find this park especially fascinating. During the rainy season, salamanders and frogs can be frequently spotted, and the park's vernal pools provide a transient but vital habitat for these and other species. The park's underbrush and canopy are home to both local and migratory species, making it a popular place for birdwatchers hoping to spot warblers, thrushes, or perhaps even a pileated woodpecker.

Resting peacefully amid the trees are Arlington's arboreal residents. The goal of Arlington's Tree Canopy Fund is to preserve and expand the city's green space, understanding that trees are essential to urban sustainability and not only beautiful features. Arlington's trees, which range in size from majestic oaks to delicate dogwoods, provide habitats, clean the air, and act as natural monuments that reflect the region's natural past. Indeed, trees make up a large portion of Arlington's population; each year, a number of "notable trees" are acknowledged officially; some of these trees have stood for hundreds of years, mute witnesses to the region's ups and downs.

For the keen-eyed observer, even the smaller parks, such as Glencarlyn Park, reveal hidden gems. From hardworking ants to elusive worms, every type of life on Earth is abundant and contributes to a complex underground ecology. As bees and butterflies fly from bloom to bloom overhead, one may hear the buzz of pollinators—a crucial natural function that, under the commotion of human activity, is usually overlooked but is critical to the survival of many plant species. Every park, creek, and tree stand contributes to Arlington's greater natural fabric by becoming a micro-ecosystem brimming with life.

Furthermore, Arlington's natural beauty is incorporated into the community's overall layout and design, not just its parks and open areas. Community gardens, green roofs, and environmentally friendly building materials are a few examples of the ways that Arlington's civic life is deeply ingrained with sustainability. While we frequently turn to the past to comprehend our origins, we also need to look up at the trees above us and down at the earth beneath our feet to recognize the live natural history that envelops us, affects our experiences, and provides a plethora of advantages, both material and immaterial.

Arlington's natural features cater to a wide range of interests, including birdwatching, hiking, and leisurely walks in the outdoors. In fact, there's something for everyone to enjoy in nature. These natural areas and animals play an active role in the community's existence rather than just serving as backdrops for human activity. They support, they educate, and—above all—they inspire. The trees and wildlife of Arlington serve as a legacy and a promise in this intricate relationship between history, culture, and environment. They are both a commitment to the future and an inheritance from the past. Arlington is both a legacy of its natural beauty and ecological resilience, as well as a result of its man-made accomplishments.

Chapter 38: Environmental Issues in Arlington

Even though Arlington is frequently praised for its attempts to combine city with nature, it hasn't been exempt from the environmental problems brought on by development and industrialization. Arlington, a heavily populated county in the Washington, D.C., metropolitan area, deals with a wide range of problems, from habitat loss and urban heat islands to water pollution and air quality. These issues are not limited to the domain of scientific research; they have significant consequences for local ecosystem health, resident quality of life, and community sustainability as a whole.

One of Arlington's ongoing major concerns is water quality. Stormwater runoff from streets and homes transfers pollutants including motor oil, pesticides, and debris into streams, such as Four Mile Run and Donaldson Run. These streams have experienced times of high contamination. The area flora and animals are negatively impacted by the deterioration of water quality, which also presents difficulties for conservation and restoration initiatives. Arlington is a riparian community along the Potomac, and its water problems are a part of larger watershed challenges that go well beyond the county's boundaries. Because of the interconnected complexity of the issue, comprehensive, multi-jurisdictional solutions are essential. To address this issue, the county has started stormwater management initiatives, green infrastructure projects, and community education campaigns.

Another issue that affects the local community but is also a regional and even global concern is air quality. Vehicle emissions are a constant worry due to the area's proximity to Washington, D.C., and important transportation arteries including Interstate 66 and U.S. Route 50. Residents who live in areas with low air quality, especially those who already have health disorders like asthma, may be seriously at risk for health problems. The goal of initiatives like the development of bike lanes, public transportation, and electric vehicle charging stations is to lessen the dependency on cars that run on fossil fuels.

In heavily populated places, the urban heat island effect is a particularly acute phenomena. This happens when heat is absorbed and reradiated by urban structures, considerably increasing local temperatures relative to nearby rural areas. Cities with higher temperatures tend to use more air conditioning, use more energy, and produce more pollutants as a result. In order to mitigate this effect, Arlington has launched a massive tree-planting effort. Trees serve as natural coolants, and the city also supports green roofs and light-colored or reflecting building materials that reflect heat instead of absorbing it.

In the meantime, the story of urban development continues to feature a depressing underbelly: habitat loss. The number of natural areas that were formerly home to local wildlife is declining or becoming more fragmented with each new subdivision or high-rise. There is an ecological and cultural imperative to protect these disappearing ecosystems since their loss not only harms biodiversity but also degrades human experience of the natural world. The Arlington County administration has taken the initiative to reserve parks and natural conservation areas, but difficulties still exist, particularly in light of the rising demand for residential and commercial real estate.

The field of social justice is also touched by environmental problems. Poorer-income areas are frequently disproportionately affected by environmental risks, such as contaminated air and restricted access to green areas. It brings up moral issues of environmental justice and equality, topics that are finding their way more and more into the larger conversation over Arlington's environmental laws.

Despite the many difficulties, Arlington stands out for taking a proactive approach and involving the community in environmental issues. Community culture of environmental stewardship is strongly ingrained, from schools implementing sustainability into their curricula to citizen-led clean-up activities.

It's like walking a tightrope when attempting to strike the delicate balance between environmental sustainability and urban expansion. However, Arlington has made a commitment to go on this trip, equipped with legislative measures, community involvement, and a sharp understanding that the environment is not only a backdrop to our lives but also an essential component of our well-being as a whole. The decisions made now will have an impact on Arlington's quality of life in the future and may even serve as a model for other cities facing comparable difficulties. Arlington's environmental problems are serious, but they also act as spurs for creativity, teamwork, and persistent action. In this chapter, we have not only outlined the problems but also offered some suggestions for how they might be resolved; every action, choice, and endeavor adds a new chapter to the continuous, dynamic tale of Arlington.

Chapter 39: Technological Advancements from Arlington

You would not immediately think of Arlington, Virginia, when it comes to technical innovation. Immediately, one could think of the legendary hubs of tech innovation, Silicon Valley in California or Route 128 in Massachusetts. But the modest state located across the Potomac River from Washington, D.C., has fostered a quietly remarkable ecosystem of technological innovations and startups of its own, supported by a densely populated area of government research facilities, a highly educated labor force, and a network of funding sources and incubators.

DARPA, or the Defense Advanced Research Projects Agency, is arguably Arlington's most notable example of technological ingenuity. DARPA was established in 1958 in reaction to the Soviet Union's Sputnik satellite launch. Since then, it has led the way in numerous significant technological developments that have altered not only military capabilities but also society as a whole. Widely extending beyond the realm of military, DARPA's impact can be seen in anything from groundbreaking work in computer networking that paved the way for the internet to developments in robotics and artificial intelligence. Arlington was a good location for DARPA because of its closeness to the Pentagon. Since then, the area has benefited from the innovative work of the agency, which has brought in top tech talent and established contractors and spin-off businesses.

But Arlington is home to more than just defense and government-sponsored projects when it comes to innovation. The county has developed into a hub for digital entrepreneurs across a variety of industries, including biotechnology, sustainable energy, data analytics, and cybersecurity. A robust network of early-stage company support organizations, such as the Ballston Innovation Initiative, and venture capital firms has made it easier to nurture these entrepreneurs. Being close to national institutions also offers special chances for public-private relationships, which are advantageous for both parties. Governmental organizations can benefit from startups' creativity and agility, and entrepreneurs can gain access to important contracts and market validation.

Moreover, the existence of academic establishments such as the Arlington campus of George Mason University has been essential in promoting an atmosphere that values research and creativity. These academic environments operate as a link between academic theory and business practice, providing a wealth of new ideas and young talent ready to make their impact on the world. Another component of the complex puzzle that keeps Arlington's technology environment alive is the practical applications that graduate research frequently finds in the business sector.

The people of Arlington are what make it a center for scientific developments, not just the institutions. Many of the county's citizens hold graduate degrees in computer science, engineering, and other tech-related industries, making it one of the most educated regions in the nation. The technical vibrancy of the region is both a cause and a result of this concentration of intellectual capital. Job possibilities in cutting-edge research and development draw people to Arlington, and their presence draws businesses and initiatives hoping to access this skill pool.

The urban planning of the area is advantageous to the technology sector as well. With its great public transportation options and compact, well-planned layout, Arlington lessens the inconvenience of lengthy journeys, promoting a lively exchange of ideas. In addition, there are several conferences, meetups, and seminars that provide venues for the IT community to congregate, exchange ideas, and work together on new projects.

Arlington has quietly but irrevocably changed the face of technology, even though it may not have the legendary reputation of more well-known tech centers. Its contributions range from defense innovations that are revolutionizing their respective industries to thriving companies that have the potential to become the next big thing. Arlington's great legacy of contributions to American technical advancement is enhanced by every new invention, successful business, and surmountable technological obstacle. In a world where technology is defining itself more and more, Arlington provides a powerful, if subtle, story of how invention may arise in the most unlikely of settings. Its tale serves as an example of what may happen when a community's special resources—whether they be in the areas of education, government, or demography—are directed toward the shared objective of technological advancement.

Chapter 40: The Future Outlook for Arlington

In light of the fact that this comprehensive analysis of Arlington, Virginia—its history, institutions, neighborhoods, and changing identity—is coming to an end, it is appropriate to cast an eye toward the future, which promises both possibilities and difficulties. Predicting the future can be a complex task when analyzing a place that is so intricately entwined with both world and American history. On the other hand, a few directional indicators can provide us with an idea of the potential paths Arlington may go in the years to come.

First and foremost, Arlington will always be a major force in politics, defense, and public policy because of its advantageous geographic location, right next to the nation's capital. Anticipate the persistence and potential growth of governmental organizations and their affiliated contractors. Given the range of 21st-century concerns confronting the United States, such as cybersecurity threats and climate change, it is reasonable to presume that Arlington will provide a friendly atmosphere for research and policy work in these sectors.

And then there's the pervasive impact of technology. Arlington has proven to be a silent force behind technology innovation, whether it comes from nimble businesses or government initiatives. Arlington may grow in appeal to tech workers and businesses looking to improve employee satisfaction without compromising career prospects as remote work continues to change the face of the workplace. This might broaden the local economy's scope. It is now strong, but it is largely reliant on defense and government spending. Younger professionals may bring with them a blossoming of cultural facilities, ranging from dining and nightlife to the arts and entertainment, thus adding to the fabric of the community.

Regarding community, Arlington's demographic fabric is expected to change as well. Even though it was already one of the most varied neighborhoods in the country, a growing number of young families and immigrants from Asia, Africa, and Latin America have moved there in recent years. Because of the influence of progressive social policies, high-quality education, and economic possibilities, this demographic dynamism is likely to persist. However, in order to preserve this diversity, the problem of cheap housing will continue to be present.

Education, which is frequently referred to as the foundation of any flourishing society, will be essential to Arlington's future. It has some of the greatest public schools in the nation, and the existence of colleges and universities fosters an innovative and lifelong learning environment. Arlington's long-term success will be greatly influenced by how it adapts its educational system to new technological and societal developments.

Sustainable principles will also be interwoven into Arlington's future. The city's decisions about how to build its policies and infrastructure for sustainable living will have an impact on the local, national, and even global arena in an era dominated by environmental issues and climate change. Arlington is already implementing programs to reduce its environmental impact, such as encouraging electric cars and sustainable urban design. The municipality is ideally positioned to be a trailblazer in the development of green technology and best practices for urban sustainability because of its tendency toward leadership in a variety of disciplines.

Let us now discuss culture, encompassing popular culture such as sports, restaurants, and festivals, as well as high culture like literature and the arts. In the upcoming years, Arlington will have the chance to reimagine its cultural identity. Its youthful population and growing diversity make it an ideal place for a vibrant arts scene, a wide range of culinary options, and a plethora of other cultural activities that enhance life in ways that go well beyond employment and education.

All things considered, Arlington's future holds a wealth of intriguing possibilities. Arlington, guided by its historical foundations but constantly adjusting to the changing demands of the contemporary world, is poised for a future that looks every bit as exciting as its history. Its particular contributions to the national and international fabric will be complemented by the convergence of government, technology, education, and community, which will continue to make it a microcosm of broader American tendencies. The stage is set for the next chapter in Arlington's evolving story, one that every new resident, tourist, and generation will contribute to creating. There are obstacles to overcome and possibilities to grasp.

Chapter 41: Must-See Locations in Arlington

Location Name	Address	Short Description
Arlington National Cemetery	Arlington, VA 22211	A solemn and revered military cemetery where notable figures, veterans, and heroes are laid to rest.
The Pentagon	Washington Blvd., Arlington, VA	The headquarters of the United States Department of Defense, offering public tours by reservation.
Iwo Jima Memorial	Arlington, VA 22209	Officially called the Marine Corps War Memorial, this iconic statue commemorates Marines who have died in combat.
Theodore Roosevelt Island	George Washington Memorial Pkwy, Arlington, VA	A walking trail system and a memorial plaza can be found in this President Theodore Roosevelt natural sanctuary.
Arlington House	Arlington National Cemetery, Arlington, VA	Once his home, the Robert E. Lee Memorial stands as a symbol of American history both before and after the Civil War.
U.S. Air Force Memorial	1 Air Force Memorial Dr, Arlington, VA 22204	A contemporary, towering building dedicated to commemorating the sacrifices and service of the US Air Force.
Signature Theatre	4200 Campbell Ave, Arlington, VA 22206	A local theater presenting a variety of shows, including musicals and dramas.
Long Bridge Park	475 Long Bridge Dr, Arlington, VA 22202	Sports fields, esplanades, and breathtaking views of the D.C. skyline may be found in this recreational park.

Location Name	Address	Short Description
Mount Vernon Trail	Starts at George Washington's Mount Vernon Estate, through Arlington	Beautiful walking and bicycling path alongside the Potomac River.
Shirlington Village	2700 S Quincy St, Arlington, VA 22206	An multitude of food, shopping, and entertainment opportunities can be found in this vibrant region.

Don't miss out!

Visit the website below and you can sign up to receive emails whenever Henry Church publishes a new book. There's no charge and no obligation.

https://books2read.com/r/B-A-GDIAB-HMMOC

BOOKS 2 READ

Connecting independent readers to independent writers.

Also by Henry Church

American Cities History Guidebook Series
Charlottesville, Virginia: Historical Guide for Travelers
Williamsburg, Virginia: Historical Guide for Travelers
Richmond, Virginia: Historical Guide for Travelers
Norfolk & Virginia Beach: Historical Guide for Travelers
Winchester, Virginia: Historical Guide for Travelers
Baltimore, Maryland: Historical Guide for Travelers
Dover, Delaware: Historical Guide for Travelers
Arlington, Virginia: Historical Guide for Travelers

About the Publisher

Northwood Lore Books is committed to publishing accessible, reflective content for curious readers.

Books in this imprint are created using a blend of human editorial guidance and AI-assisted writing and editing technologies. Authors use pen names and are not certified subject-matter experts.

All works are for educational or entertainment purposes only and should not be considered financial, legal, medical, or other professional advice. Consult appropriate professionals before relying on the information contained within.